Phrasal verbs in conversation

COLIN MORTIMER

Longman

LONGMAN GROUP LIMITED
London

Associated companies, branches and representatives throughout the world

© Longman Group Limited 1972

First published 1972
*New impressions *1973; *1974; *1975; *1976*

ISBN 0 582 52217 X

Printed in Hong Kong by
The Continental Printing Co Ltd

TO MY MOTHER

During the academic year 1966–7, I had the good fortune to study for a year
in the Departments of English Language and Phonetics in the University
of Leeds. I should like to acknowledge my debt to the staffs of those departments, and to hope that, with all its imperfections, this little book will be
accepted by them as a modest but serious attempt to manifest some of what
I was taught at Leeds about language in general and about phrasal verbs
and collocation in particular.

I should like also to record, with thanks, my debt to the British Council's
English Language Teaching Institute, in London, which has been a constant
and unique source of inspiration, practical, expert guidance, and invaluable
experience.

Lastly, I wish to express my gratitude to my wife for her shrewd, construc-
tive comments on individual dialogues, and to her and my two children for
having surrendered so cheerfully, while the book was being written, so
much time that was rightfully theirs.

Introduction

This book of 432 conversations is intended for upper intermediate and advanced students of English as a second or foreign language. It is also suitable for private study, and as a reference work for teachers. It can be used intensively or extensively as a component of a course, or as supplementary practice material.

Aims

1 To contextualize individual meanings of a large number of phrasal verbs in such a way that these meanings will be remembered. Each conversation attempts to present a dramatic and developing situation with economy of words, and with some attention to compelling rhythmical and stylistic patterning. The situations are fairly adult and are based particularly on the workings of human nature – a powerful source of motivation in language learning that has often been left untapped in language teaching materials.
2 To supply groups of words that regularly accompany particular phrasal verbs and that should be learnt in company with them. These groups of words help to limit and define the meaning of a verb.
3 To give practice in the use of phrasal verbs in context, and with appropriate lexical company.
4 To serve as a complement to a dictionary of phrasal verbs or to the definitions of phrasal verbs entered in conventional dictionaries.
5 To act as a source of comprehension, interpretation and composition work. Some of this work will arise from the implicatory nature of many of the dialogues. These leave something significantly *unsaid* in order that something still remains to be said by the student – who, it is hoped, will then feel impelled to make explicit, in speech or writing, what is only implicit in the text.
6 To simulate some of the characteristics of spoken, as opposed to written English, and to give practice in the use of the spoken form.
7 To provide material for acting purposes.

A NOTE ON PHRASAL VERBS

The English Language has hundreds of two part verbs such as 'bring up', 'carry on' and 'put up'. These are easy enough to understand when the meaning of the whole two part verb is equal to the meaning of the sum of its two parts: we can understand what 'bring up a table' means, provided we know the meaning of 'bring' and the meaning of 'up'.

But in many cases knowing the meaning of the parts does not help us to know the meaning of the whole. Thus, to add the meaning of 'bring' to the meaning of 'up' will not help us to understand the meaning of 'bring up' in the expression 'He brought up a point'. Nor will it help us to understand 'bring up' in the expression 'She brought up a family'.

These uses of 'bring up' are *idiomatic*. To understand their meanings, we may, perhaps, need dictionary definitions; but above all we need to meet the verbs, and remember them, in the kind of context in which they are used, and in which we might ourselves use them. And we need to learn the groups of words that regularly accompany particular verbs. Thus, 'bring up', as in 'bring up a point', is also often accompanied by 'question', or 'issue', or 'matter'. On the other hand, 'bring up', as in 'bring up a family', can be accompanied by 'child', 'son', 'grandson', 'orphan', etc.

We could say that in the paragraph above, we have two meanings of the single verb 'bring up'. But in this book it is suggested that it is more useful to *think of each separate meaning as a separate verb*, which is to be considered separately, learnt separately in one's mind, along with the situation in which it is met, and the lexical company it regularly keeps.

Thus, it is useful to think of 'blow up' in 'blow up a bridge' as one verb, 'blow up' in 'blow up a balloon' as a second verb, 'blow up' in 'blow up with anger' as a third verb, 'blow up' in 'the.storm blew up' as a fourth verb, and 'blow up' in 'blow up a photograph' as a fifth verb – each of these to be learnt separately.

Each of the conversations in this book is devoted to one separate meaning of one phrasal verb. Each of the verbs is idiomatic (though some are less idiomatic than others), and each is an adverbially particled verb. Thus, even though 'go through' as in 'go through an experience' is idiomatic, it is not met in this book, because it is prepositionally particled. Such idiomatic verbs are often called 'prepositional verbs' to distinguish them from phrasal verbs – which are adverbially particled idiomatic verbs.

We can sometimes tell whether a transitive verb is a phrasal verb or whether it is a prepositional verb by the position the pronoun takes. Thus we can 'bring up a point' and we can 'bring it up': but when we 'go through an experience', we 'go through it', we do not 'go it through'.

Also, the adverbial particle in a phrasal verb is often separable, but the prepositional particle in a prepositional verb is not separable. We can 'bring up a point' and we can 'bring a point up'; but though we can 'go through an experience', we cannot 'go an experience through'.

Intransitive two part idiomatic verbs – 'blow over', for example – are, of course, phrasal verbs, and many of these are included in the book.

Most of the verbs used in this collection have been selected because most of their meanings are frequently encountered. Some, such as 'blow up' as in 'blow up a photograph', have been chosen because they are beginning to be widely used and will almost certainly be used increasingly.

Phrasal verbs are *used* a great deal, especially in spoken English. So it is important for a student to recognise their meaning at least. If he wants to learn to speak English naturally and well, however, he must try to use these verbs himself – once he understands them properly. It is possible to use few of these verbs in one's speech; but then one is likely to sound rather formal, and possibly a bit pompous – 'enter' for instance, is a rather more momentous verb than 'come in', and is not always appropriate to the same occasions.

The verbs in this book are arranged in alphabetical order so that, if he so chooses, the student can use the book as a complement to, or amplification of, the dictionary.

THE CONVERSATIONS

The more the conversations are used and discussed *as conversations*, and as a source of comprehension and composition work, the more effectively will they fix in the mind of the student the meaning and use of the particular verbs on which they focus.

Each conversation should first be tackled as a whole. It can either be presented as a prepared reading or performance by the teacher and one of the best pupils (perhaps twice, or even three times), or it can be treated as a reading comprehension. After general questions such as 'What's it about?' have been answered, the conversation can be gone through more carefully, more detailed questions on content can be asked, and new constructions and vocabulary can be dealt with.

Most of the conversations thrust one into a situation in the very first line. Many of them suggest that something has happened before the dialogue begins, and at the end they often imply what will happen afterwards. As well as answering straightforward comprehension questions, the student can speculate about what happened before, what is implied during, and what will transpire after the conversation. He can also decide who the speakers are, discuss their characters, and suggest what their relationship to each other is. He can try to relate the situation presented in the dialogue to his own experience. For example, in the first conversation the student can say whether he or she has ever been embarrassed in a restaurant or other public place by a companion, and if so how and where, and what the outcome was.

It may be that the student will not always be able to express accurately *in* English the implications that he has apprehended *through* English. If his English is good enough to give him the insights, but not sufficiently developed for him to express these insights, then he can use the mother tongue first, and the appropriate interpretative English can be arrived at by intelligent stages.

One of the important features of this book is the attempt made to simulate the constructions, repetitions, interruptions and hesitations used in spoken English. Hesitations often merit interpretation; interruptions result in unfinished sentences – and it is useful for the student to supply the words that would have been uttered had there been no interruption. For example, in 'Put off (v)', the speaker interrupts *himself*: 'He's a fool and he's a nuisance, and what's more, he's a . . . Ah, Mr Pratt!'

The dialogues can be repeated aloud, first in chorus, or in two groups, and then in pairs. Then they can be acted at the front of the class either with book in hand, or from memory. Many of them lend themselves even to public performance. Selections can be presented in quick succession as a means of displaying the prowess in English of a whole class.

Memorizing the dialogues is a useful exercise, but it is important, also, in the later stages, to give the student an opportunity to 'free' the language in the dialogue and to use it in a consonant, normalized situation arising from his own experience.

As the process of reading, listening, comprehension, discussion, explanation, performance and composition goes on, the relevant phrasal verb is used many times and, directly and indirectly, its formal features are dealt with. One's hope is that during the process, meaning has been 'rememberably' imparted.

THE DRILLS

After each conversation there is a drill which quotes from the conversation one or two lines involving the use of the phrasal verb that is featured. These lines should be drilled first in chorus, then in groups and then in pairs, for pronunciation practice, and to fix the idiom. In some of the quotations, the particle is included in brackets in two positions to indicate that two versions of the sentence are possible.

For example: He hasn't added up this bill correctly.
He hasn't added this bill up correctly.

It should be noted, however, that though the particle *can* often be used in two positions, this does not mean that, in natural speech, it always *is* used equally often in the two positions, or that to use it in one rather than the other position does not sometimes cause a slight shift in meaning or emphasis. Until more research has been done into the subject, experience must be our guide here.

When the quoted lines have been drilled, they can be varied by referring to the substitution columns below them. Selected words or phrases in the quotations are in bold type to indicate that the items listed below them can be put in their place:

e.g.   I'm going to break (up) the **furniture** (up)
chairs
table
bed

It should be noted that the use of bold type is in no way an indication of stress, and is only used to show that substitutions are possible. Sometimes an item in the quotation – such as a proper name or a number – is printed in bold type even though no substitution list appears below it. In these cases the student is invited to supply his own substitutions – e.g. for John, the names of other people in the class.

When a sentence quoted from a dialogue is varied by reference to the substitution lists, the new sentence produced will retain the *meaning* of the phrasal verb as used in the dialogue on which it is based; it will not, however, always necessarily reflect the actual *situation* presented in the dialogue.

The following are some of the sentences that can be constructed from the drill and lists that accompanies 'Break up (i)':

A What do you intend doing with that hammer?
B I'm going to break up the table.
A I see.

A What are you thinking of doing with that chopper?
B I'm going to break the bed up.
A I see.

A What do you intend to do with that axe?
B I'm going to break up the chairs.
A I see.

It is suggested that such a phrase as 'I see' is not only conclusive and useful, but also satisfying to say, and it acts here as a constant in a varying sequence, rather like a refrain in song or verse. Rhythmical and stylistic patterning is probably far more relevant to learnability than, perhaps, writing for language teaching purposes has so far taken into account.

THE TAPES

The book is accompanied by three tapes on which 124 dialogues are recorded. The conversations are spoken at normal speed: they have not been said in the especially deliberate style that is often employed in tapes for teaching purposes. While there may be a slight loss in clarity, there is a considerable gain in naturalness. Appropriate hesitations, repetitions and interruptions are included.

These tapes are an extensive source of listening and pronunciation practice. But they are also much more than this. They are not mere 'readings aloud' of the written texts, but are also *interpretations* of them. As such they add a dimension of meaning to the texts. Thus, for instance, in 'Buy over', the speaker's tone on the phrase 'You get them for nothing' suggests, perhaps, not only worldliness, but in addition an element of world weariness. In 'Lock up', A's tone on 'Goodnight' indicates perhaps that having said 'Good night' to her on many previous occasions, it is only at this particular moment that he has actually noticed her. In 'Break up (i)' there is a pause before the phrase 'I see'. The student should interpret this pause in terms of the bewilderment the speaker must have experienced before he said 'I see'. 'I see' also occurs in 'Make up (iv)'. In this conversation, it probably means that the speaker, having seen an example of Mr Ross's work, has no intention of ever having a suit made by him. It also indicates the speaker's opinion of B's judgement and taste.

In their quest for stylistic and rhythmical, as well as human interest, and in seeking to include an interpretable component, these conversations attempt to make some contribution in that area where language for teaching purposes and the language of literature can and should meet.

It is suggested that each conversation should be listened to as a whole — once, twice, or several times, with or without the text. Then questions of a general nature can be asked about it. Next, the tape can be played through a speech at a time for more specific comprehension questions. After this, the conversation can be played once more, and pauses can be made (using the pause device on the tape recorder) for repetition in chorus, in groups, and individually.

For example: William, I know we've been extravagant (pause), but please don't spoil our anniversary (pause), etc.

If necessary, the extracts can be repeated: dextrous and accurate rewinding comes quickly with practice. Sometimes it is a good idea to read the written text first and decide on one's own interpretation of the characters and situation before listening to the taped version. And sometimes it is interesting and productive to present a tape without the text and to stop it after each speech, or even a part of a speech, so that, if the text has not been seen at all, the student can try to predict what the next speech, and, ultimately, the outcome of the whole conversation is going to be.

After each recorded dialogue, the quotations used in the drill are recorded, with a pause for repetition. When these lines have been repeated a few times, it is hoped that the tunes of these sentences will be retained in the student's mind as a guide to the stress and intonation of the further sentences that he makes up with the help of the substitution items.

The pauses on the tape for repetition purposes are only very slightly longer than the utterances that are to be repeated. This quick 'pacing' is intentional: a short pause indicates the time in which the utterance can and should be said by the advanced student, unless his delivery in his own language is rather slow;

it also helps a student gradually to get the feel of the rhythm of English and to repeat with the correct rhythm. Too much time to consider is, perhaps, inimical to good rhythm. On the other hand it is appreciated that some students may be discouraged or made nervous by too short a pause, or find it demands too much of them at their present level of attainment in pronunciation. The answer to this difficulty lies in the pause key, or button, or lever, which practically all tape recorders have. By pressing the pause key after a sentence, one can extend the pause for repetition for as long as one likes. One can *extend* a pause, but unfortunately one cannot *shòrten* a pause so easily. A long pause breaks up the rhythm of the tape, and many students are bored by longer pauses – they lose the feeling of being impelled into the kind of repetition that gives a sense of participation.

The pauses on the tape, then, have been made intentionally short in the knowledge that a properly controlled pause key can make them just as long as one likes.

Many of the conversations on the tape do, of course, lend themselves to extended development in the language laboratory: listen and repeat, role playing, pattern drills, transformation drills, etc.

Dialogues that have been recorded on the three tapes that accompany the text are asterisked * in the text.

Some of the dialogues are spoken with a slightly regionalized pronunciation, where such a pronunciation seems to be appropriate. Dialogues which have been recorded with this slightly non-standard pronunciation are marked **. In these cases the taped version of the dialogue is perhaps more for interpretation and listening purposes than for imitation. Even so, imitating a non-standard pronunciation is good practice occasionally, provided that one realizes what one is doing.

add up*

A. William, I know we've been extravagant. But
please don't spoil our anniversary. Don't add
up the bill in that ostentatious manner –
people will stare.
B. But he's added it up wrongly!
A. Oh, William! Are you sure you've checked it
carefully?
B. Waiter, you haven't added this bill up
correctly!
A. He hasn't heard you. Promise not to make a
scene, William, please!
B. Waiter! Waiter!!
A. Oh, William!
B. I say! Waiter!!

(b) He hasn't added (up) **this**   **bill** (up) **correctly**.
                       these   columns properly
                               figures
                               totals
                               items
(a) Are you sure you've checked **it** carefully?
                                      them

ask out

A. Shall I ask Susan out to the theatre?
B. She doesn't like the theatre.
A. Shall I ask her out to a restaurant?
B. She doesn't like restaurants.
A. Shall I ask her out to the cinema?
B. She doesn't like films.
A. I see! Well, shall I ask her out to . . .
B. And she doesn't like you.

(a) Shall I ask **Susan** out to **the theatre**?
                              a restaurant
                              the cinema
                              a dance
                              celebrate
(b) She doesn't **like**   **the theatre**.
                enjoy   restaurants
                        films
                        dancing
                        celebrating

1

back up* A. I know I'm the right man for the job; and I realize I have the best claim to the job. But I shan't get it without someone to back me up.
B. Won't Johnson back up your claim? Surely he'll back you up?
A. Why should he? Johnson wants the job himself.

(a) I shan't get the **job**   **without**   **someone** to back me up.
            post   unless I have   somebody
            appointment   if I haven't
            part
            contract
            commission
(b) Won't **Johnson** back you up?

barge in A. You weren't invited! Nobody asked you to come! They were all behaving themselves until you came barging in!
B. Barging in?
A. You'd no right to barge in!
B. I'd every right – it's my flat, isn't it?

(a) They were all **behaving themselves** until you came barging in!
              enjoying themselves
              perfectly happy
                      contented
                      well-behaved
                      quiet
(b) Barging in?
(a) You'd no **right**   **to barge in!**
            reason
            excuse for barging in

2

bear out   A. I wouldn't have believed the story myself until a week ago. But this evidence of yours bears out another report I've had.
B. Well, 'there's no smoke without fire' – as the proverb says!
A. And I'm afraid the rumour's borne out further by this tape-recording – listen.

(a) This **evidence** of yours bears out another **report** I've **had**.
information		got
testimony		received
news	rumour	heard
	story	

(b) Well, 'there's no smoke without fire'!
(a) And the report's borne out further by this **tape-recording – listen**.
photograph	look
photostat	
letter	
document	see
file	
dossier	

bear up*   A. You know, there's absolutely no need to be depressed. Do try to bear up, please!
B. That's what they all say: 'Try to bear up,' they say, 'try to bear up'!
A. Well, please, won't you just try?
B. But I have tried! Of course I've tried! And I know I've no good reason to feel depressed. But I am depressed, and that's all there is to it! So please, everybody, do stop telling me to bear up – it only makes matters worse.

(a) **You know**, there's absolutely no **need** to be **depressed**.
Actually	reason	unhappy
Believe me		gloomy
		dispirited
		melancholy
		sad

Do try to bear up.
You must
You really should
You ought to
(b) Please, **do stop** telling me to bear up! It only makes matters worse.
  don't keep on
  don't always be

3

beat down A. You say it's a bargain? Hm! A bargain, you say? You should've beaten him down a bit.
B. I did beat him down.
A. You should've beaten him down to £3.
B. I beat him down to £1.
A. You should've . . . to £1? Hem! Er . . . well, I still say you were robbed!

(*a*) **You** should've beaten **him** down.
He   them
(*b*) I did beat **him** down.
He   them
(*a*) **You** should've beaten **him** down to **three pounds**.
He   them   four dollars
(*b*) I beat **him** down to one **pound**.
He   them   dollar

beat off A. Tom's terribly boring. He's always talking about the war. He never stops talking about his army days. He's a dreadful bore!
B. He won a medal, you know.
A. No, I didn't know.
B. Yes, he beat off an enemy attack single-handed. All his comrades were dead. Reinforcements hadn't arrived. But Tom managed to beat the enemy off all on his own.
A. Funny – I've never heard him mention that.

(*b*) He beat off the **attack**   **single-handed**.
                    onslaught   all on his own
                    offensive   all by himself
                    enemy
                    forces
(*a*) **Funny** – I've never heard him **mention** that.
     Strange   refer to
     That's odd   talk about

beat up
(i)

A. There! Three eggs. Now I'm going to beat up the mixture with my fork.
B. Mother will be furious when she comes in!
A. How long should I beat it up, do you think?
B. You can beat it up until your arm drops off for all I care – it'll be a ghastly cake, anyway!

(a) Now I'm going to beat (up) the **mixture** (up) with my **fork**.
                               ingredients   whisk
                               batter
(b) Mother will be **furious** when she **comes in**!
                   very cross   gets back
                   angry   comes back
                   wild   comes home

beat up
(ii)

A. Well, as I said, the bandits stopped the lorry, and they beat up the driver dreadfully. I wasn't beaten up quite so badly.
B. And your mysterious passenger? Did they beat him up too?
A. No. As a matter of fact he beat them up. That's why nothing was stolen.

(a) The **bandits** beat (up) the **driver** (up) dreadfully.
         thieves   guard   terribly
         robbers   policemen very badly
         gangsters   victim
         hi-jackers   driver's mate
(b) **And you?**
    What about you?
    What happened to you?
(a) I wasn't beaten up **quite so badly**.
                  too badly
                  very much
                  much at all

block up
  A. Stop!
  B. But I want to drive in.
  A. You can't. The entrance's been blocked up.
  B. But it can't've been blocked up. I live just over there. I always come this way.
  A. Well it has been blocked up.
  B. Who's blocked it up?
  A. I have.

(a) The **entrance's** been blocked up.
      gateway's
      passage's
      path's
      road's
      way's
      track's
(b) Who's it been blocked up by?
(a) **By me.**
    Me.

blow out
  A. Now, where are the matches? I'll light the candles on the cake. One, two, three, four, five .... There! Now, Margaret, you must blow them all out.
  B. But I want to blow out the candles!
  A. Stop it! You mustn't! It isn't your birthday, John, it's Margaret's. Margaret, dear, go on – blow really hard. That's the way! What a clever girl! Well done! Now we'll cut the cake. Shall we let him help us to eat it, if he's good? Or shall we eat it all ourselves?

(b) I want to blow (out) the **candles** (out)!
                            match
                            taper
(a) **Stop it!** It isn't your birthday, **John**, it's **Margaret's**.
    Stop that
    You mustn't

blow up
(i)*

A. They're enjoying themselves. It's a marvellous party. Can I do anything to help?

B. Well, I've blown up nearly all the balloons. Yes, this lovely red one's the last. You can blow it up if you like.

A. Ah! I'm rather good at blowing balloons up.

B. Don't blow it up any further! It'll burst! There, what did I tell you?

A. Hem! Yes. Er . . . ah. Well, can I do anything else to help?

(a) Can I do anything to help?

(b) Well, I've blown (up) **nearly** all the balloons (up). You can blow this up, if you like.

almost
practically
just about

(a) Ah! I'm **rather** good at blowing balloons up.

quite
pretty

blow up
(ii)

A. It's calm now. But what will happen if a storm blows up?

B. If a storm blows up, we shall get wet.

A. And the boat?

B. The boat'll get wet too. But don't worry – it won't sink.

(a) But what will happen if a **storm** blows up?

wind
gale
hurricane

(b) If a **storm** blows up, we shall **get wet**.

wind
gale
hurricane

ride it out
signal for help
say a prayer

7

**blow up
(iii)**

A. Don't be a fool! Can't you smell the fumes?
If you light a match, the whole place will
blow up!
B. It needs blowing up!
A. But not with me in it, thank you very much!

(a) If you **light**   **a match**   the whole **place** will blow up!
                      the fuse   ship
      press   the button   cellar
                     the plunger   installation
        pull   the trigger   tank
(b) It **needs**   **blowing** up!   arsenal
     wants   to be blown
     deserves

**blow up
(iv)**

A. Yes, we have enough explosive to blow up the
bridge.
B. Good. We'll clear the area. Clear the whole
area! Clear it! They're going to blow the
bridge up! They're blowing it up in fifteen
minutes!

(a) Yes, we have enough **explosive** to blow (up) the **bridge** (up).
                          high explosive   building
                          dynamite   house
                          T.N.T.   machine
                          gelignite   tunnel
(b) Clear the whole area! They're going to blow (up) the bridge (up)!

blow up
(v)

A. This photograph shows his head and shoulders. Do you think you could blow up his left eye?
B. Let me see. Mm, the negative's quite good. Yes, it's quite a sharp negative. A really big enlargement should be possible. Yes, I think we can blow it up for you. You say you want a blow-up of his left eye?
A. That's right, yes – the left eye.

(a) Do you think you could blow (up) **his left eye** (up)?

right thumb

this face in the crowd

the number of this car

this part of the picture

photo

(b) Yes, I **think** we can blow **it** up for you.

expect   that

suppose   this

imagine

reckon

blow up
(vi)

A. John, I'm sorry I blew up just now.
B. Nonsense – you had every reason to blow up. I shouldn't have done such a stupid thing.
A. But I'm supposed to have such a sweet temper!

(a) **John,** I'm sorry I blew up **just now**.

a moment ago

yesterday

last night

(b) **Nonsense** – you had **every reason** to blow up.

Rubbish   every right

Don't be silly   good reason

Think nothing of it   a perfect right

                     every excuse

(a) But I'm supposed to have such **a sweet** temper!

an even

book up

A. What about Thursday? Could we go then? They say it's a marvellous play.
B. I should think all the seats'll be booked up. And anyway, I'm booked up myself next week.
A. I've telephoned the theatre. The seats aren't all booked up, in fact.
B. Well, as I've just said, I am booked up.
A. If that's the way you feel, I'll ask Tom if he'll take me.
B. That's right. You ask Tom.
A. Oh, you exasperate me!

(a) The **seats** aren't all booked up, **in fact**.

tickets	actually
places	in actual fact
vacancies	as a matter of fact

(b) Well, **as I've just said**, I am booked up.

as I say
as I've told you

(a) Oh, you **exasperate me**!

infuriate me
make me cross

break down (i)

A. Can you come quickly, please? Everyone's in a dreadful panic.
B. Whatever's wrong?
A. Oh, everything's broken down: the computer's broken down, the adding machine's broken down – even the typewriters've broken down. Oh, and by the way, I'm afraid you'll have to come down by the steps.
B. The lift?
A. Yes, I'm afraid it has!

(b) **Whatever's wrong**?

What's wrong
What's the trouble
What's the matter

(a) Oh, the **computer's** broken down.

machine's
engine's
car's
clock's
lift's

10

**break
down (ii)**

A. Now why don't you be sensible? The house is surrounded. Open the door, or we shall have to break it down.
B. Break it down, if you like!
A. All right, men, break the door down!
B. By the way – it isn't locked, you know.

(a) We shall **have to** break (down) the **door** (down).
     be obliged to fence
     be forced to   barrier
            partition
(b) Break it down, **if you like**.
     if you want to
     if you want
     if that's what you want to do
     by all means

**break
down (iii)**

A. These statistics look very encouraging, until you break them down.
B. What do you mean?
A. Well, if you break down this total, for instance, you'll see that it includes stock we are going to throw away.
B. So what do you want me to do?
A. I want you to do a breakdown for me of all the totals.

(b) So what **do you want** me to do?
    would you like
(a) **I want** you to break (down) these **totals** (down) for me.
  I'd like   figures
         statistics
         numbers
         items

**break
down (iv)**

A. The negotiations broke down last time. Do you think this meeting will fail too?
B. Yes, I think these negotiations will break down, just as the others did.
A. Do you really think so?
B. Yes I do. Surprisingly, you know, both sides seem to want them to break down.

(a) Do you **think** the **negotiations** will break down?
          reckon   talks
                    discussions
(b) **Both sides**   **seem to** want them to break down.
    The two sides appear to
        delegates
        delegations
        participants

**break
down (v)**

A. That was the year he broke down, of course. It's surprising how many people in his job do have nervous breakdowns, isn't it?
B. And it was so terribly tragic, I remember. He was getting ready for a world tour. It was so sad to see him in that condition. I admit, I almost broke down and wept myself.
A. But now he's all right.
B. But he had to change his job, of course.

(a) He broke down **under the strain**.
                because of stress
                through over-work
(b) It was so sad to see him in that **condition**. I admit, I **almost** broke down
                              state   nearly
                                       practically
                                     very nearly

    and **wept** myself.
        cried

break off (i)

A. What a lovely bar of chocolate!
B. Daddy gave it to me. I'm going to break a piece off for you, and a piece for John. And I'm going to break off two squares for daddy – because he bought it.
A. You are a kind little girl. And you're very strong!
B. And I'm going to eat all the rest myself.

(a) What a lovely   bar of   chocolate!
        beautiful   toffee
                        nougat

                        candy
            stick of barley sugar
                      liquorice
                      rock

(b) I'm going to break (off) a piece (off) for you.
                      square   mummy
                    two pieces   John
                      squares

(a) You are a kind little girl.
            nice   boy
            good

break off (ii)

A. Now isn't that interesting?
B. Isn't what interesting?
A. He's broken off the talks about the new contract, and he's broken off his engagement to Jenny – all on the same day! However, I think the talks will probably resume next week.
B. And the engagement?
A. If I know him, that won't be broken off permanently, either!

(a) The talks have been broken off.
    discussions
    negotiations
(b) And his engagement to Jenny?
(a) He's broken that off, too.
                as well

break off (iii)

A. You poor, poor man! But surely you didn't work all that time without a break?
B. Oh, no. At eleven, we broke off for coffee. At one o'clock we broke off for lunch – er ... for an hour and a half. We had tea at four, of course. And just after five, we had a drink, and then broke off altogether. By the way – is there a cup of tea?
A. There will be – when you've made it!

(*a*) But surely you didn't work **all that time** without a break?

> for all that time
> for all those hours
> for over seven hours

(*b*) **Oh, no.** At eleven we broke off **for coffee**.

Oh, certainly not	for lunch
Of course not	for a smoke
Of course we didn't	for a drink
	altogether
	for good

break out (i)

A. There's been another gaol-break!
B. How many've broken out?
A. It says here that five prisoners broke out this afternoon, but three of them were recaptured almost immediately.
B. And the others?
A. Smith and Reilly!
B. Smith and Reilly? They've broken out before, haven't they?
A. And they'll break out again!

(*a*) They've broken out of **prison** again.

> gaol
> the detention centre
> remand home
> police station
> top security wing
> their cells

(*b*) How many've broken out?
(*a*) **Five**.

14

break out (ii)

A. It must be something they've eaten.
B. Have they actually been sick?
A. No, but John's broken out in spots, and Margaret's broken out in a dreadful rash.
B. And what about you?
A. Oh, I'm perfectly all right. But when I saw John's spots, I did break out in goosepimples. I'll confess! I was terrified!

(b) Have they actually been sick?
(a) No, but John's broken out in **spots**.
> pimples
> a rash
> a dreadful rash
>   terrible
>   nasty
>   an awful

(b) And **what about you**?
> how about your husband

break out (iii)

A. I read in the newspaper there's been another outbreak of violence in . . .
B. There's always something, isn't there?
A. If it isn't fighting that breaks out, it's fire that breaks out, and if it isn't fire that breaks out, it's a new epidemic that breaks out, and if it's not . . .
B. Still, it does give us something to talk about, doesn't it? I remember that on the day the war broke out, I was . . .
A. I think I'll just go out for stroll.

(a) It isn't **a war** that breaks out . . .
> fighting
> violence
> trouble

(b) It's **a fire** that breaks out.
> 'flu
> measles
> an epidemic
> disease

15

break out (iv)

A. Did you have a good week?
B. Well, for the first few days it rained and rained – it was awful! And then, suddenly, on the Tuesday, the sun broke out. And after that, it was a beautiful week.

(*a*) Did you have **a good week**?
        nice weather
(*b*) Well, **suddenly**, on the **Tuesday**, the sun **broke out**.
    quite suddenly   Friday   broke out from behind a cloud
    all of a sudden

And after that, it was a **beautiful** week.
        lovely
        gorgeous
        delightful

break up (i)

A. What are you going to do with that axe?
B. I'm breaking everything up. I've already broken up the bed and the dressing-table in there. Now I'm going to break this table up, and the chairs, and all the rest of my furniture.
A. I see.
B. Here's a hammer. Would you like to help?
A. You're very kind. But I think, if you don't mind, I'll just sit down for a moment!
B. But not on that chair, please.

(*a*) What **are you going to do** with that **axe**?
        thinking of doing   chopper
    do you intend doing   hammer
                       sledge-hammer
(*b*) I'm going to break (up) the **furniture** (up).
                chairs
                table
                bed
(*a*) I see.

break up

(ii)

A. When do the children break up for the holidays?

B. I think they break up on the last Friday of the month – they did last year.

A. Those dreadful Fisher children have broken up already, I see.

B. They've broken up, yes – but their school hasn't.

(a) When do the children break up for the **holidays**?
  end of term?
  Christmas holiday?
  summer holiday?

(b) I think they break up **tomorrow**.
  next week.
  on the twentieth.

(a) Those **dreadful Fisher** children have already broken up.
  awful   Smith
  horrible

break up

(iii)

A. It was a good meeting.

B. What time did it break up?

A. Oh, at about ten.

B. Did the police have to break it up this time?

A. No they didn't. For once, it broke up peacefully of its own accord.

(b) Did the police have to break (up) the **meeting** (up)?
  party
  crowd
  demonstration

(a) No they didn't. For once it broke up **peacefully** of its own accord.
  quietly
  uneventfully
  without incident

bring about

A. What brought it about? What caused the misunderstanding?
B. Well, for one thing, he introduced too many changes too quickly.
A. But we do need a change of attitude here. We need a change of heart. Surely you agree about that.
B. Oh, I agree with you there.
A. And if he can't bring it about, who can?
B. You can.

(b) He brought about a lot   of **misunderstanding**.
               certain amount   disagreement
                              dissatisfaction
                              unwelcome changes
(a) We need **someone** to bring about **a change of attitude**.
         somebody   change of heart
                          some changes

bring back

A. Well, I'll say goodbye, then, Mr Brown.
B. Goodbye, Headmaster. And thank you for letting me come. You know, my visit has brought back my schooldays so clearly. And it's brought back many, many memories.
A. Happy ones, I hope.
B. Most of them happy, and I was thinking . . . Ah! School dinners! The smell of school dinners!
A. And what sort of memories does that bring back, Mr Brown? Or would you rather not say!

(b) My visit has brought back **my schooldays** so clearly. And it's brought
                                  youth
                                  the past
                                  the old days
                                  those years
back **many, many** memories.
    so many
    a host of
    lots of
(a) Happy ones, I hope.

18

bring off* A. If he manages to bring off the deal, what will you do?
B. If he does manage to bring it off, and does win the contract – and that's a very big 'if' – I shall er . . . I shall recognize his services, of course.
A. Mm. And if he doesn't bring it off?
B. If he fails to bring this one off, I shall have to dispense with his services.

(a) If he doesn't bring (off) the deal (off), what will you do?
(b) If he **doesn't** bring it off, I shall **dispense with his services**.

      fails to   ask him to resign
                               ask for his resignation
                               sack him
                               give him the sack

bring on* A. Oh, do stop fussing, dear!
B. But grandmother, you know that too much excitement brings on your palpitations, and I think you really ought to go to . . .
A. I'm not going back to bed. People die in bed! I'm going down to your party, and what's more, I'm going to dance – even if it does bring my palpitations on. Now, where's my scent?

(b) But you know that too much **excitement** brings (on) your **palpitations** (on).
                              noise   attacks
                              strain   headaches
                                             asthma
(a) I'm going to **dance**, even if it does bring **them** on.
          go down   it
          enjoy myself
          the party
              dance
              ball

bring out (i)

A. We certainly are bringing out a new edition of our cookery book, but we're not quite sure when it'll be ready for publication.
B. I hear your rivals have recently brought out an entirely new cookery book.
A. Mm. I've seen it. But it isn't really new, of course. In fact, you might call it mutton dressed as lamb!

(b) **I hear** your **rivals** have brought (out) **an entirely** new **cookery book** (out).
　　believe　　competitors　　　　　a completely　dictionary
　　I'm told　　　　　　　　　　　　　　　　　　　　atlas
　　They say　　　　　　　　　　　　　　　　　　　encyclopaedia
　　　　　　　　　　　　　　　　　　　　　　　　　course
　　　　　　　　　　　　　　　　　　　　　　　　　series

(a) But it isn't really new, **of course**.
　　　　　　　　　　　　　　you know
　　　　　　　　　　　　　　you understand
　　　　　　　　　　　　　　to be quite frank

bring out (ii)

A. Yes, I did enjoy his lecture. And I think that a slightly sceptical audience brings out the best in him.
B. Perhaps you're right. Even so, I thought he was a bit obscure. What did he mean by the word 'idrealism', by the way?
A. Ah, you must read his latest book! The meaning of 'idrealism' is brought out very clearly in the first chapter.

(a) Such **an audience** brings out **the best in him**.
　　　　a subject　　　　　　worst
　　　　situation　　　　　　his worst side
　　　　question　　　　　　his best side
　　　　　　　　　　　　　　qualities

(b) What did he mean by the word '**idrealism**', by the way?

(a) The meaning of that word is brought out very clearly in his **latest** book.
　　　　　　　　　　　　　　　　　　　　　　　　　　　　new
　　　　　　　　　　　　　　　　　　　　　　　　　　　　recent

bring out (iii)

A. Jeremy was so shy, you know. But school has really brought him out. He's just as lively and noisy as the rest now.

B. And Michael starts school tomorrow.

A. Yes, he does. But, of course, I'm not at all worried about Michael. He needs no bringing out! Quite the reverse, in fact.

(a) **School** has really brought **him** out.
Going to school   John
Starting school
(b) And **Michael** starts school tomorrow.
(a) **He needs no bringing out**! Quite the reverse, in fact.
She doesn't need any bringing out
      doesn't need to be brought out

bring round (i)

A. I know you feel dreadful at the moment. But I assure you a bit of fresh air will soon bring you round.

B. It'll take more than fresh air to bring me round. And in the circumstances, I think you should order some drinks, and pay for them!

A. But it was all in the cause of science, you'll agree.

B. Maybe so. But I'm not going to be one of your guinea-pigs again, I can tell you!

(a) **A bit of fresh air** will   **soon** bring you round.
    breath of fresh air   quickly
    drink of water
    drop of this medicine
    spoonful of this mixture
  One of these pills
  This injection
(b) It'll take more than **fresh air** to bring me round.
               water

bring round (ii)

A. This morning none of them would agree with me. But now, I think, I've brought most of them round to my point of view.

B. Even so, you'll have to bring all of them round, won't you?

A. Well, actually, I was hoping that you might persuade the rest – they're women, you know.

(a) I've brought most of them round to my **point of view**.
                    way of thinking
                    view
                    position

(b) Even so, you'll **have** to bring **all of them** round, won't you?
              need   them all

(a) Well, actually, I was hoping that you might persuade **the rest**.
                        the others
                        the remainder

bring to

A. I've slapped him, and I've splashed water on his face – but it hasn't brought him to.

B. And it won't bring him to, I'm afraid.

A. What are you doing?

B. Pulling this blanket over his face.

(a) I've **slapped him**, but it hasn't brought him to.
           splashed water in his face
           opened the window
           given him an injection
                  artificial respiration
                  the kiss of life

(b) And it won't bring him to, **I'm afraid**.
                        I regret to say
                        I'm sorry to say

bring up (i)*

A. Well, ladies and gentlemen, that concludes our meeting – that is, unless there's any other business.
B. May I bring up just one more point? It really must be brought up, I think you'll agree.
A. At our next meeting, if you don't mind.
B. Ah ... er ...

(b) May I bring (up) just one more **point** (up)?
　　　　　　　　　　　　　matter
　　　　　　　　　　　　　issue
　　　　　　　　　　　　　question
　　　　　　　　　　　　　subject
(a) **At our next meeting** – if you don't mind.
　　Next time
　　　　week
　　　　month

bring up (ii)*

A. Your grandmother brought fifteen children up. Didn't you, dear?
B. What's that you say?
A. Fifteen children. You brought up fifteen, didn't you?
B. I did. I did indeed! And I brought them up properly! I brought up seven boys and eight girls.
A. She did.
B. Or was it eight boys and seven girls?

(a) She brought (up) **fifteen children** (up).
　　　　　　　　　　　sons
　　　　　　　　　　　daughters
　　　　　　　　　　　nieces
　　　　　　　　a big family
　　　　　　　　　large
(b) And I brought them up **properly**!
　　　　　　　　　　　correctly
　　　　　　　　　　　very well

23

bring up
(iii)*

A. Well-brought-up children don't 'bring up' their food.
B. But auntie, I have brought it up.
A. You've done no such thing – you've been 'ill'.

(*b*) But **auntie**, I have brought (up) my **food** (up).
    granny   dinner
                                    jelly
                                    ice-cream
(*a*) You've done **no such thing** – you've been 'ill'.
               nothing of the kind   unwell

brush up

A. 'Brush up your languages using the latest instruction techniques. Cash refunded if not delighted.'
B. The trouble is, I've neither languages to brush up, nor cash to be refunded.
A. So you want a course for absolute beginners?
B. For absolute, penniless beginners!

(*a*) 'Brush (up) your **languages** (up).'
                  French
                  Maths
(*b*) The trouble is, I'**ve no languages** to brush up.
              haven't any French
                       Maths

build up
(i)

A. I can remember when there were no houses here. No shops. Just fields, and the cliffs, and the sea.
B. And now the area's completely built up, except for your bit of land.
A. Yes, apart from my bit, it's been built up for the last ten years, at least.
B. Mrs Thompson, it was your piece of land I wanted to talk to you about.

(b) Now the **area's** **completely** built up.
    place entirely
    district
(a) Yes, apart from my **bit**, it's been built up **for the last ten years**.
      piece   past
      plot   since 1960
      patch

build up
(ii)

A. I just don't understand you, Nigel. You've been here fifteen years, you've built up a very good practice, you've built up a fine reputation, and now, suddenly, you want to learn an entirely new job. It doesn't make sense!
B. To me it makes sense.
A. Well, it won't make money, I can tell you that.

(a) You've built up **a very good practice**. It doesn't make sense!
        fine business
        first class organization
      an excellent
      a fine reputation
        name
        name for yourself
(b) **To me it makes sense**.
 It makes sense to me
 To me it does

build up
(iii)

A. Naturally, he's lost a great deal of weight, and he's lost a bit of confidence. He'll need building up both in spirits and in body, you know! Do you think you can do it, Mrs Roberts?

B. I'll build him up in no time, don't you worry, doctor.

A. I'm sure you will. Well, here he comes now.

(a) He'll need **building up**, you know.
　　　 to be built up
(b) I'll build (up) his **spirits** (up) in no time, **don't you worry**.
　　　 confidence　　　　　　leave it to me
　　　 morale　　　　　　　 you can be sure of that
　　　 muscles

butt in

A. Sorry to butt in, Mr Bartle, but your wife is on the telephone.

B. Don't apologize, Miss Myers. Anyway, we weren't talking about anything special, were we, Terence? Excuse me, won't you?

A. I was so sorry to butt in – you seemed so engrossed in conversation with him.

B. But I was rather glad to be interrupted. You see, Terence was just about to ask for a loan.

(a) **Sorry to butt in, Mr Bartle.**
　　　 for butting in
　　　 Forgive me for butting in
　　　 Forgive my butting in
(b) **Don't apologize, Miss Myers.** Anyway, we weren't **talking about** anything
　　　 No need to apologize　　　　　　　　　　　　　 discussing
　　　 Think nothing of it

　　　 special.
　　　 in particular
　　　 of importance

26

butter up* A. He doesn't give interviews at all. You know that yourself.

B. You must flatter the old boy, butter him up a bit. Tell him he has a duty to posterity.

A. I don't believe in buttering people up. Why don't you try to persuade him?

B. Hm! He won't listen to me!

A. Oh, well, of course, if he won't listen to the cleverest and most highly respected man in our business, how can you expect him to listen to a mere beginner like me?

(*b*) **You must** butter **the old boy** up a bit.
You'll have to   fellow   little
                        chap
              our client
              customer
              your husband
              the boss
(*a*) **I don't believe in** buttering people up.
        hold with
        like
   dislike
   hate

buy out   A. I do the work and make all the decisions.
(i)   He's the sleeping-partner in this firm – and that's how I like it.

B. Why don't you buy him out?

A. It might be a good idea some time. But at the moment, I haven't the money. Besides, even if I offered to buy him out, he might refuse. And what's more, if I did offer to buy him out, my sleeping-partner might very well wake up!

(*b*) **Why don't you** buy **your partner** out?
Why not offer to   boss
                          father
              the other shareholders
(*a*) Even if I offered to buy **him** out, **he** might **refuse**.
                          them   they   say no
                                          reject the offer
                                          turn the offer down

27

buy out (ii)

A. To cut a long story short, my son was so angry about my decision, that he went away and joined the army.

B. Have you heard from him?

A. Yes – he's written to say he'll forgive me if I'll change my decision and if I'll buy him out.

B. So you'll change your decision?

A. Oh, no – I shan't change my decision. And I shan't buy him out of the army, either!

(*a*) **He'll forgive me**, if I'll buy him out.
    He's willing to forgive me
        prepared
(*b*) So **you'll**   change your decision?
      have to
    you're going to
(*a*) Oh, no – I shan't change my **decision**. And I shan't buy him out of the
                                  mind
    army, either!
    infantry
    artillery
    air force
    navy
    forces

buy over*

A. All we need now is a respectable Chairman. He must be a distinguished public figure – and Porritt is our man!

B. You think he can be bought over, just like the others?

A. Bought over? A man like Porritt? You don't buy men like Porritt over, Wilfred! Men like Porritt can't be bought!

B. Well, then, how are we . . .

A. But if you go the right way about it, you get them for nothing!

(*b*) You **think** he can be bought over, just like **the others**?
    reckon   rest
                          all the others
                                rest
(*a*) **You don't buy** men like **Porritt** over, Wilfred!
    One doesn't buy
    No one buys
    Nobody can buy

buy up   A. They're gradually buying up all the property in the district.
B. And they're buying up all the shares on the market. It's dreadful, isn't it?
A. They want to buy my business up.
B. I offered them mine. But they wouldn't have it!

(a) **They're gradually** buying (up) all the **property** (up).
   Bit by bit they're   shops
   Slowly but surely they're   houses
                                land
                                businesses
                                shares
(b) I offered them mine. But they **wouldn't have it!**
                        didn't want them
                        refused
                        weren't interested

call in   A. Did he stay long?
(i)   B. No, he said he'd just called in about the rent.
A. Is he coming back?
B. He said he'd call in again later this evening.
A. What time?
B. At about seven.
A. Ah.
B. What shall I tell him this time?
A. Why not come with me instead?

(b) He said he'd just called in **about the rent**.
                            some money
                      to ask you something
                      to see you for a moment
                      to have a word with you
(a) **Is he coming back**?
   Did he say if he was coming back
   When's he coming again
   What time's he coming back
   How soon's he coming back
(b) He said he'd call in again **later this evening**.
                    later on
                    a bit later on
                    sometime tomorrow
                          in the morning

call in
(ii)

A. Yes, sir, I see your point. But only the first five hundred models were defective. We've called those in and we've corrected them. The others don't need calling in – they're perfectly all right.

B. What about mine, though? It's only number 501, you see.

A. Yours was the first of the new batch.

B. Are you quite sure of that?

A. Quite, quite sure, sir. You've nothing at all to worry about, sir. (To himself) I know what we'll do next time this happens!

(a) We've called (in) the **defective** models (in).
　　　　　　　　　　faulty
(b) What about **mine**?
　　　　　　my car
　　　　　　my vehicle
(a) Yours was the first of the **new batch**.
　　　　　　　　　　　　　lot

call in
(iii)

A. Very well, then, spend the money! Call in the experts! Call a firm of consultants in! Call in the police, or a doctor, or even a clergyman, for all I care!

B. But surely you must agree that a second, expert opinion would be valuable.

A. I don't know about valuable. It would certainly be expensive.

B. But it would tell us . . .

A. And it wouldn't tell us anything that we don't know far too well already.

(a) **Very well**, then, call (in) **the experts** (in)!
　　All right　　　　　　　a firm of consultants
　　　　　　　　　　　　　some specialists
　　　　　　　　　　　　　a public relations firm
(b) But you must surely agree that a second, **expert** opinion would
　　　　　　　　　　　　　　　　　　　specialist
　　　　　　　　　　　　　　　　　　　professional

　　be **valuable**.
　　　　invaluable
　　　　very useful
　　　　a good idea
(a) I don't know about **valuable**. It would certainly be expensive.

30

call off (i)**

A. You can call off the search. In fact, you can call off the whole operation – we've found him.

B. I'll let the family know.

A. Tell them not to call the wedding breakfast off – it'll do for a funeral tea, won't it? See you later.

B. Yes, see you later. (To himself) I suppose he's what you might call a professional – a real, hard-bitten professional. Or perhaps he's just been in the job for too long. Ah well!

(a) You can call (off) the **search** (off).
    operation
    investigation
    wedding
    celebrations
    reception

(b) I'll let **the family** know.
    parents
    relatives
    her father
    his mother
    the next of kin

call off (ii)*

A. Call him off, can't you?

B. He's only doing his duty, Ernest.

A. Well, if that's the way you feel, I'll go away, and I won't tell you about the new sports car I'm buying.

B. Oh, Ernest, you think of a new story every time! I'll call him off in a minute. But first you must give him time to say 'Good morning' properly.

A. Call him off! Call the great, clumsy, slobbering creature off!

B. Oh, Ernest! You do look sweet!

(a) Call (off) your **dog** (off) can't you?
    hounds
    guard-dogs
    bodyguards
    men

(b) **He's** only doing **his** duty, **Ernest**.
    They're   their

31

**carry on
(i)****

A. I tried to be polite to her, and I tried to be patient with her. But, d'you know, she carried on just like a baby! Just like a baby, she carried on! 'It's too hard for me!' she shouted. 'I can't do it, and I won't do it, and you can't make me do it!' she screamed. Oh, dear me, what a carry on it was!

B. I know. I've heard her carrying on like that myself. But she'll grow out of it.

A. I'm glad you think so!

(a) D'you know, she carried on **just like a baby**!
　　　　　　　　　　like a child
　　　　　　　　　　like a two year old
　　　　　　　　　disgracefully
　　　　　　　　　in an awful way
　　　　　　　　　in a shocking manner

(b) I've heard her carrying on like that myself.

　　But she'**ll grow out of it**.
　　　　　won't always be like that
　　　　　　　　behave like that

**carry on
(ii)**

A. Well, as I said, cups and saucers were rattling in the kitchen, and there was a dog barking outside – but he carried on playing his flute, just as if nothing had happened. And the audience were entranced!

B. Oh, you don't need to tell me about my husband! Last week, he was supposed to be cooking a chicken for me. The house was absolutely full of smoke, and the smell of burning was terrible. But he carried on practising his flute!

(a) He carried on as if nothing had happened.
(b) He carried on **practising his flute**.
　　　　　　　　playing his violin
　　　　　　　　reading his book
　　　　　　　　writing letters
　　　　　　　　cleaning the car
　　　　　　　　repairing the roof

carry on (iii)

A. Mm. He'd carried on that business reasonably successfully for, oh, twenty years at least.
B. And you say he was operating an international crime syndicate while carrying on a perfectly legitimate business here?
A. That's it. But then, suddenly, his legitimate business began to be, legitimately, too successful, and then . . . well, he became rather careless about the syndicate.
B. Fifteen years, would you say?
A. Oh yes, he'll get fifteen at least. Maybe more.

(b) He was carrying on a **perfectly legitimate** business.
                    sound
              well-established
              very profitable
                  successful
(a) Mm. He'd carried it on successfully for, oh, **twenty years**
                                              ten   months

    at least.
    at the very least

carry on (iv)*

A. Everything in order?
B. Yes, sir.
A. Carry on, sergeant. Everything in order, corporal?
C. No, sir.
A. Carry on, corporal.
C. Sir?
A. Carry on.
C. Yes, sir.

(a) Everything in order?
(b) Yes, sir.
(a) Carry on, **sergeant**.
       corporal
      Lieutenant Smith
      Private Brown

carry out

A. He's bluffing. Don't take any notice.
B. But if he carries out his threat, I'll be ruined.
A. He won't carry out his threat, as long as you carry out my instructions. Now listen carefully. This is what you must do.

(b) If he carries out his **threat**, I'll be ruined.
　　　　　　　　　　　plan
　　　　　　　　　　　promise
　　　　　　　　　　　intention
(a) He won't carry it out. Now **listen carefully**.
　　　　　　　　　　　　　　pay attention

　This is what you must do.
　　　　　　　I want you to do
　　　　　　　I think you should do
　Here's what　　　　ought to do
　　　　　　　　　　need to do

carry through (i)

A. I agree that he initiated the whole programme, and I agree that he had the vision.
B. And surely that's what matters. It's the vision that matters.
A. Maybe so. All I'm saying is that most of the sheer hard work of carrying the reforms through was done by someone else. And I doubt very much if they could've been carried through without that man. And we both know very well who I mean, don't we?
B. Well, I er . . . it's er . . . it's very nice of . . .
A. You underestimate yourself, you know.

(b) That's what matters. It's the **vision** that matters.
　　　　　　　　　　　　foresight
　　　　　　　　　　　　insight
(a) **Maybe so.**　　　But I doubt if the **reforms** could've been carried
　Perhaps so　　　　　　　　　　programme
　Maybe you're right　　　　　　　plan
　Perhaps　　　　　　　　　　　policy

　through without **that man**.
　　　　　　　one man
　　　　　　　you

carry through (ii)

A. It was his indomitable courage that carried him through, doctor. He's a very brave man.
B. It wasn't only his courage that carried him through, Mrs Curran – it was the thought of you, you know.
A. Oh, doctor.
B. Anyway, as I said, he's naturally very tired. However, in you go. But only for a few minutes, mind!

(a) It was his **courage** that carried him through.
             fortitude
             patience
             determination
             sense of humour
             strength of mind
(b) It wasn't only his **courage** that carried him through, **Mrs Curran**.

catch on (i)

A. I look absolutely ridiculous in them! Take my word for it, these 'trousers,' as you call them, will never catch on. I'm certainly not going to equip my army with them, even for the invasion of Britain. And you can take it from me, the public will never buy them.
B. Well, of course, you have the last word. But, believe me, stranger things than trousers have caught on, you know, Julius!

(a) **Take my word for it**, **trousers**'ll never catch on.
   Take it from me   shirts
                     the fashion
                        style
                     the idea
                     that
                     your
(b) Believe me, stranger **things** have caught on!
                    fashions
                    styles
                    ideas

catch on (ii)*

A. But didn't he recognize your voice on the telephone?

B. No – I disguised it. I spoke like this: 'Smithers? This is the Chairman.' And then I told him to expect a promotion soon.

A. Didn't he realize it was a practical joke? Didn't he catch on?

B. No he didn't. And I don't think he's caught on yet. If he has, he's keeping very quiet about it.

A. Come to think of it, I had a telephone call from the Chairman the other day.

(a) Didn't **he** catch on?
    she
    Sam
    Joy

(b) I don't think **he's** caught on yet. If **he** has, **he's keeping**
    she   she   she

                                                   not telling anyone
                                                                anybody
                                                   not saying anything
                                                   keeping it to himself
    very quiet about it.
    extremely

clean out (i)**

A. I expect you'll want to start work as soon as you can. But, as I said, I've occupied this office for almost forty years, and, well, I've er . . . I've . . . accumulated such a lot of rubbish, I'm afraid. So much rubbish. I think I shall need another day or so to clean it all out.

B. Yes, there is a lot of rubbish, isn't there? The place certainly does need cleaning out.

A. It needs cleaning out, as I said, yes. But it's not all rubbish, you know.

(a) I shall **need**   **another day or so** to clean it all out.
          require a few more days
                  a bit longer
                  a little more time

(b) It certainly **does need cleaning out**.
                 needs   to be cleaned out

clean out (ii)

A. I'm sorry, but I'm completely cleaned out at the moment. I haven't a penny to my name.

B. But it was only £1!

A. Even so, I'm flat broke. Cleaned out entirely. And anyway, you know very well I don't believe in lending money. It's the principle of the thing.

B. I don't want to borrow it – you owe it to me!

A. I suppose you say that to all your victims!

(a) I'm **completely** cleaned out **at the moment**.
entirely	just now
utterly	just at present
quite	just at the moment

(b) But it was only **£1**!
£3
50p
two dollars

(a) Even so, I'm cleaned out. I haven't a **penny** to my name.
cent
sou

clear off*

A. Clear off, the lot of you!

B. But we only wanted to wish you 'Many happy returns of the day', grandfather.

A. I know very well what you wish me – and it isn't many happy returns. Now, clear off, before I send for my shotgun!
And if you really want to know, I'm leaving it all to charity – every last penny of it. So you needn't come any more, need you?

(a) Clear off, **the lot of you**!
all of you
every one of you

(b) But we only wanted to wish you **many happy returns**.
a happy birthday
anniversary
a safe journey
a pleasant trip
a speedy recovery

(a) Clear off, before I **send for my shotgun**.
gun
the police
call my dogs
set my dog on you

37

clear up
(i)

A. Can I clear up the mess now?

B. No, this room hasn't been examined for fingerprints yet. But we've finished downstairs – you can clear up downstairs, if you like.

A. Thank you, officer.

B. And you'll remember my advice, won't you?

A. Oh, yes, officer, of course I'll remember. (To herself) I suppose what he says about jewel cases is perfectly true. But, honestly, whoever could bear to keep their jewels in a cornflakes packet? Really!

(*a*) Can I clear (up) the mess (up) now?

(*b*) You can clear up **downstairs**, if you like.

> the kitchen
> > sitting-room
> > dining-room
> > other rooms
>
> upstairs
> your bedroom
> the bathroom

clear up
(ii)

A. A drop of rain never did anyone any harm. Let's go, shall we?

B. I'm going to wait for it to clear up.

A. But we can't stand in this doorway all day. And it isn't going to clear up for ages. Look at those clouds. Let's be brave, shall we?

B. You can be brave, if you like. I prefer to be dry.

(*b*) I'm going to wait for it to clear up.

> the weather

(*a*) It isn't going to clear up **for ages**.

> > a long time
> > some time
> > quite a bit
> > a while

clear up (iii)*

A. Here's John. Perhaps he can clear up the mystery.
B. What mystery?
A. It's this object, John. What's it for? What's its purpose?
B. Ah! I can soon clear that little mystery up for you! The fact is, it hasn't got a purpose, and it doesn't need to have a purpose. It's a work of art!
A. Oh! Well, thank you for telling me. I was going to put it in the bathroom.

(a) Perhaps you can clear (up) the mystery (up).
                                this difficulty
                                problem
(b) I can soon clear (up) that little mystery (up).
      quickly   difficulty
                                  problem

close down

A. That's it, of course. Now I remember. And, surely, just around this corner is Mrs Church's Bakery.
B. Not any more, I'm sorry to say. The bakery closed down, oh, five or six years ago, I should think. Mrs Church died, you know.
A. No, I didn't know.
B. You'll find that a lot of the old businesses have closed down.
A. Ah, but here's one that hasn't! What about a drink before lunch, Edward?

(b) You'll find that **a lot** of the old **businesses** have closed down.
                           a number   shops
                           many   firms
                           a large number places
                           great
(a) But **here's** one that hasn't!
      there's
      that's
      this is

close in**   A. It's quiet, isn't it?

B. That's the trouble – it's too quiet.

A. You think they're . . . closing in now?

B. They're closing in, all right! And in a
moment, they'll attack. Sh! Did you hear
that?

A. An owl.

B. Have you ever heard of owls in these parts?

(*a*) You **think**   they're closing in now?
        reckon the enemy
               raiders
               police
               soldiers

(*b*) They're closing in, **all right!**
                  you can be sure of it
                           certain of that
                  there's no doubt about it
                                     that
                  without a doubt

close up   A. If we close up this footpath, then people will
(i)   stop interfering with the crops.

B. I'm afraid we're not allowed to close it up –
it's a public footpath. People have a perfect
right to use it. If you wanted to close it up,
you'd have to ask the permission of . . .

A. I'm closing the path up now. And I'll answer
questions later.

(*b*) **I'm afraid** we're not **allowed** to close it up.
      sorry but   permitted
    Unfortunately

(*a*) I'm closing (up) the **path** (up) now. And I'll answer questions later.
                 track
                 road
                 entrance
                 alleyway

close up
(ii)

A. When they stood in line outside their block, the six prisoners closed up, you say . . .
B. Yes, they closed up, sir, so that the seventh fellow couldn't be seen from the front.
A. So how did you know he was there?
B. The sun was low in the sky, sir.
A. And?
B. And I counted the shadows, sir.

(a) The **six prisoners** closed up, you say.
    men
    soldiers
    cadets
    guards
(b) **Yes**, they closed up, sir.
    That's right
    That's it

clutter up

A. Mr Battersby, I have told you until I'm tired of telling you that this is a laboratory – it isn't a menagerie, and it isn't a whisky distillery. I will not allow you to clutter up the place with all this . . . with all this cluttter!
B. Yes, the place is a bit cluttered up with one thing and another, Mr Boffin, I agree. Er . . . perhaps you'd help me to make a start by accepting one of Tabby's new kittens.

(a) I **will not allow** you to clutter (up) the place (up).
    refuse to
        permit
(b) Yes, the **place** is a bit cluttered up, **Mr Boffin**, I agree.
    laboratory   admit
    office   it's true
    room   you're quite right

come down (i)

A. I remember you had your villa by the sea, and your big, white car, and your jewels and your clothes and . . .

B. And now I can hardly afford a taxi, and I live here in this . . . in this place. Yes. Yes, I suppose I have come down in the world a bit. I must've come down, mustn't I? Otherwise I wouldn't be talking to someone like you, would I?

(a) I remember you had your **villa by the sea**.
        big, white car
        expensive clothes
        exquisite jewels
(b) Yes, I **suppose** I **have** come down in the world **a bit**.
        admit   must've   somewhat
        confess

come down (ii)

A. It is a very wise saying, I agree. And in my book, I've included similar proverbs that have come down to us from even earlier times – this one, for instance.

B. But, of course, you mustn't believe everything grandfather tells you, even in his book. Most of his proverbs have come down from ancient times, as he says. But I suspect that some of them have come down only from . . .

C. She thinks I invent them in my bath.

B. Well, admit it, you do invent some of them in your bath.

C. Really, how can you say such a thing! 'Too many baths spoil the book,' you know. That's a very old proverb!

(a) In my **book** I've included similar **proverbs** that have come down to us
        article   sayings
        survey   stories
        dissertation   traditions
                                             customs
    from **even earlier times**.
        prehistoric times
(b) But you mustn't believe **everything grandfather tells you**!
                            all   says

42

come

down (iii)

A. You promised that your prices would come down before the end of the year.

B. Our prices certainly would've come down if the cost of living – and our cost of production – hadn't gone up.

A. But you gave an assurance that . . .

B. Yet, despite these considerable increases in costs, our prices haven't actually increased.

A. But you guaranteed that . . .

B. Which, in the circumstances, is the same as saying our prices have, in fact, come down. Isn't it?

(a) You **promised** that your **prices** would come down.
gave an assurance   charges
guaranteed   fees
                    rates

(b) Our **prices** certainly would've come down, if the cost of **living** hadn't
charges   production
fees   labour
rates   materials

     gone up.

come

off (i)

A. It's such a lovely play. Really, you must see it soon, or you'll miss it. It comes off at the end of this month to make way for a new thriller, you know.

B. That play's been running at the same theatre for over two years now. Every time the audiences get a little bit smaller, the management spread the rumour that it's coming off soon.

A. But it really is coming off this time.

B. Why should I care?

A. Well, I would like to see it just once more.

(a) The **play** really is coming off **this time**.
production   soon
film   shortly
opera   in the near future

(b) **Why should I care?**
Why should I worry
It doesn't bother me
I couldn't care less

(a) But I would like to see it just **once more**.
                                 one more time

come off (ii)

A. When does the wedding come off, then?
B. I don't know now if it ever will come off.
A. But surely you and Jennifer haven't changed your minds?
B. No, but we've changed our jobs.
A. What difference does that make?
B. It makes about a hundred miles difference. And a hundred miles can make all the difference in the world, can't it?

(a) When does the **wedding** come off, then?
    engagement
    party
    celebration
(b) **I don't know** now if it ever will come off.
    I can't say
    I'm not sure

come off (iii)

A. It was an amateurish performance, but it certainly came off, didn't it? Everyone thought it was a marvellous success.
B. Yes, it came off very well.
A. Perhaps these newcomers have something to teach us after all, eh?
B. Only that we're not as young as we were – and, of course, we know that already, don't we?
A. You speak for yourself!

(a) The **performance** certainly came off, didn't it?
    production
    play
    film
    programme
    idea
(b) Yes, it came off **very well**.
    marvellously
    wonderfully
    admirably
    completely
    without a doubt

44

come on

(i)

A. Come on! Do hurry up – we're going to be late.

B. I just want to check the back door.

A. Oh, do come on!

B. Yes, that's locked.

A. Come on, hurry up – or it won't be worth going to!

B. (To himself) It won't be worth going to, anyway. All right, I'm coming!

(a) Come on! Do hurry up – we're going to be late.
(b) I just want to **check the back door**.
                 find my key
                 put (out) the cat (out)
                 turn (out) the lights (out)
(a) Oh, do come on!

come on

(ii)*

A. We don't often see you at this time of day, headmaster.

B. Well, it's such a delightful morning, Mr Smith, isn't it? How's the garden, by the way?

A. Oh, as you can see, the vegetables are coming on well.

B. And the flowers?

A. Mm, they're coming on quite nicely too.

B. Good, good. Well, actually, Mr Smith, I was wondering if I might have a word with you about William.

A. About William. Yes. Yes, William isn't coming on at all well, is he, headmaster? Perhaps we'd better go into the house.

(b) **How's the garden**?
    How are the flowers
                 vegetables
                 roses
                 carrots
(a) **It's** coming on **well**.
    They're   quite nicely
                 reasonably well
                 fairly satisfactorily
(b) And **William**?
(a) He isn't coming on at all well.

45

come on
(iii)

A. It was a perfect day to begin with, so neither of us took a coat or umbrella, or anything.
B. And then the storm came on quite suddenly.
A. We were absolutely drenched! (Sneezes)
B. Bless you!
A. And I think I have a cold coming on.

(*b*) And then the **storm** came on **quite suddenly**.
     rain   all of a sudden
     cold weather slowly but surely
     winter
(*a*) And I think I have **a cold** coming on.
        fever
        'flu

come out
(i)

A. Don't worry about him – worry about yourself.
B. Yes, but he's so depressed about the examination, you know. When the results come out, I really don't know what he'll do he might even . . .
A. When the results come out, you'll find that he's done better than you have. I know him! And I know you!

(*b*) When the **results** come out, I really **don't know** what he'll do.
    marks   can't imagine
    grades
    percentages
(*a*) When they come out, you'll find he's done better than **you have**.
              you've done
              you

come out (ii)

A. Do you think the men will actually come out on strike, or are they bluffing?
B. Oh, I think they probably will come out.
A. And us?
B. If they strike, I think we'll be asked to come out in sympathy with them.

(b) I think they probably will come out on strike.

I think	the men	possibly
	the workers	almost certainly
	that firm	
	department	
	factory	
	company	

(a) And us?
(b) We'll be asked to come out in sympathy with them.

come out (iii)

A. When does your new book come out?
B. It's come out already – do you mean to tell me you haven't bought a copy?
A. Do you mean to tell me you haven't saved a complimentary copy for me?
B. Yes, I have saved you a copy, but not a complimentary one.
A. Oh, all right! How much? By the way, you are coming to our Dinner Dance, aren't you?

(a) When does your new book come out?
novel
anthology
collection
(b) It's come out already. Do you mean to tell me you haven't bought
ordered
borrowed
a copy?

47

come out
(iv)

A. Did everything come out exactly as you planned?
B. Not exactly, no. As a matter of fact, things came out rather better than I'd planned.
A. He signed the contract, then?
B. No, she signed it.
A. It was a she?
B. It was a she – and I've invited her out to the theatre this evening. And she's accepted!

(a) Did **everything** come out **exactly** as you **planned**?
it all	just	hoped
		expected
		intended
		wanted

(b) **As a matter of fact**, things came out **rather** better than I'd **planned**.
Actually	somewhat	hoped
To be quite honest	a bit	
To tell you the truth	a little	
	a lot	
	much	

come
round (i)

A. This lump feels as big as an egg.
B. It looks as big as an egg. How long were you unconscious before you came round?
A. My head's still buzzing – I'm not altogether sure I have come round yet. But I know he hit me at exactly two minutes past three.
B. How do you know the exact time?
A. Because he hit me with the clock! And, as you can see, it stopped at two minutes past three precisely!

(b) How long were you unconscious before you came round?
(a) I'm not **altogether sure** I have come round yet.
exactly	certain
quite	positive
really	

48

come
round (ii)

A. He's a stubborn old fool.
B. What you mean is that he doesn't agree with your plan.
A. That's it – he's a fool.
B. If I were you, I'd try not to be in too much of a hurry. He'll come round to your way of thinking, in time.
A. He'll come round in time, you say. But that's the trouble – I haven't got any time!
B. What you mean is that you haven't got any patience!

(b) He'll come round to your **way of thinking in time**.

point of view	due course
viewpoint	a while
view	soon
	before long

(a) But **that's the trouble** – I haven't got any time!
  difficulty
  problem
  annoying thing
  irritating
  But that's just *it* –

cool down

A. If you'll just cool down for a minute, I'll explain.
B. Stop telling me to cool down!
A. But if you'd just stop losing your temper, and cool down for a moment . . .
B. I am not losing my temper!!
A. And if you'd stop shouting for a second or two . . .
B. I AM NOT SHOUTING!!!

(a) If you'll **just** cool down for a **minute**, I'll explain.
  only   moment
                                second
                                while
                                bit

(b) **Stop** telling me to cool down!
  Don't keep
  Can't you stop
  Why do you keep on
  Must you always be

cover up*　A. They don't like people who make mistakes. He made a mistake.
B. And he tried to cover it up.
A. Shall we say he failed to cover it up.

(b) He **tried** to cover (up) his **mistake** (up).
　　 attempted　　　　　　　 error
(a) **Shall we say** he failed to cover it up.
　　 One might say
　　 You

crop up*　A. Something important's just cropped up at the office, Janet. So I shan't be able to meet you for lunch after all, I'm afraid.
B. I don't know! Whenever you arrange to take me out to lunch, something always crops up. What is it this time?
A. I have to meet an important buyer at the airport.
B. And take him out to lunch, I suppose.
A. And take her out to lunch, I'm afraid.

(a) Something important's just cropped up **at the office**.
　　　　　　　　　　　　　　　　　　 at home
　　　　　　　　　　　　　　　　　　 at work
　　　　　　　　　　　　　　　　　　 at the works
　　　　　　　　　　　　　　　　　　 in our department
(b) What is it this time?

50

dash off

(i)

A. She left in rather a hurry, but before she dashed off, she left this note for you.

B. Let's see . . . 'Your dinner's in the oven, the table's laid, and the kettle's on – sorry, but I must dash.' Mm. She doesn't say where she's dashed off to, or when she'll be back. Or even if she'll be back.

A. Oh, she'll be back. She hasn't taken the canary with her!

(*a*) Before she dashed off, she **left** this **note** for you.
                       gave me   message
                                     letter

(*b*) Mm. She doesn't say where she's dashed off to.

dash off

(ii)

A. It takes me ages to write a letter, whereas John can dash off half a dozen in an hour.

B. So he writes all the family letters.

A. I said he can dash them off in an hour, when he wants to. The trouble is, he doesn't often want to.

(*b*) So **John writes all the family letters.**
            deals with all the correspondence
            handles all the letter writing

(*a*) He can dash (off) **half a dozen letters** (off) in **an hour.**
                  lots of letters   a very short time
                  all our correspondence   next to no time
                                       no time at all

The trouble is, he **doesn't often want to.**
                very rarely wants to

die down   A. This scandal will ruin him!

B. You mustn't underestimate either him or his powers of recovery. The scandal will die down as soon as the newspapers get a new front page story. And when all the fuss has died down, he'll be back – not necessarily in the same place, or with the same name, or even with the same face. But he'll definitely be back, believe me.

(a) This **scandal** will ruin him.
       rumour
(b) The **scandal** will **soon** die down. And when all the **fuss** has died down,
       rumour   quickly   excitement
                                                 noise
                                               hullaballoo
                                               ballyhoo

    he'll be back, **believe me**.
                take it from me
                take my word for it

dig up   A. He seems to be a very reliable man.

B. Yes. But if you ask me, he's a bit too good to be true. I want you to check on him. Make extensive enquiries. See what information you can dig up about his life during the last ten years.

A. Actually, I've already dug up one rather interesting fact.

B. About his career?

A. About his hair.

B. He hasn't got any – he's bald, like me.

A. Yes, but whereas you wear your wig all the time, he only wears his outside office hours.

(b) See what **information** you can dig up about him.
           facts
(a) I've already dug (up) one interesting **fact** (up).
                                  thing
                                  item
                                  reference
                                  photograph
                                  letter
                                  piece of evidence
                                            information

do in

(done

in) (i)

A. I am tired, of course, yes. In fact, I'm absolutely done in – we're all done in. But a good night's sleep is all we need.

B. And do you think you can finish the job by tomorrow evening?

A. Finish it tomorrow? We've finished it today – that's why we're all so done in.

(a) I'm absolutely done in.

(b) Can you **finish** the **job** **tomorrow?**
    complete   work tomorrow morning
                     soon
                     in the near future

(a) We've **finished it today** – that's why we're all **so** done in.
    already finished it   completely
                                           absolutely
                                           quite

do in

(ii)**

A. He's dead.

B. I always knew someone would do him in. He was a blackmailer. He deserved to be done in.

A. And where did you find this little book?

B. In his pocket. Those are the names of the victims.

A. Someone's torn a page out, I see.

B. Why should anyone want to do that, I wonder?

A. You didn't tear it out, I suppose?

B. I didn't do him in, if that's what you mean.

(a) **He's** dead.
    Smith's

(b) He deserved to be done in. He was **a blackmailer**.
                                        an extortioner
                                        a crook
                                          murderer
                                          thief
                                          swindler

doze off*
A. What time is it, then?
B. Nearly midnight.
A. Oh dear! I must've dozed off. This is such a comfortable chair. Did you have a nice time?
B. Lovely, thank you. Grandfather, you've burnt another hole in your jacket! And you promised not to smoke any more cigars in that chair.
A. And I've kept my word, my dear. I was smoking when I dozed off – but it was only a cigarette.

(a) **What time is it**, then?
   What's the time
(b) Nearly **midnight**.
(a) **Oh dear!** I must've dozed off.
   Dear me!
   Gracious me!
   Really?
   Is that so?

draw aside
A. In front of the other guests, he said he was going to resign. Then he drew me aside, and told me, in a whisper, and in the strictest confidence, that he wasn't going to resign at all.
B. Beware of James when he draws you aside and whispers in your ear in the strictest confidence.
A. What do you mean?
B. James never confides in anybody. He tells his secrets only to those ... only to those who won't keep them.

(a) He drew me aside and told me his **secret**.
                              plans
                              decision
                              real intention
                              motive
(b) Beware of **James**. He **never confides in anybody**.
              doesn't confide in anyone
              confides in no one

54

draw out
(i)

A. I'm afraid I've drawn out £100.
B. Well, it's your money – you've a perfect right to draw it out.
A. Yes, but I haven't got anything like £100 in my personal account.
B. So you're overdrawn?
A. So I drew it out of our joint account.

(a) I'm afraid I've drawn (out) **£100** (out).
(b) It's your money. You've **a perfect right** to draw it out.
            every right
(a) Yes, but I haven't got anything like **£100** in my **personal** account.
                                                own
                                                current

draw out
(ii)

A. He's usually such a very concise speaker – why do you think he's giving such a long drawn-out explanation of this particular point?
B. I don't know. Perhaps he's drawing it out to try to convince himself it's true.
A. Or perhaps he's trying to bore us all so much that some of us will go away.
B. And, then, of course, he'd be able to introduce his new plan with less opposition.

(a) Why is he drawing (out) his **explanation** (out) so much?
                                story
                                report
                                speech
                                introduction
(b) Perhaps he's **trying** to bore us all **so much**   that **some of us** will
                  intending   to such an extent a lot of us
                  hoping   many of us
                                                              most of us
                                                              all of us
                                                              everybody
                                                              everyone

        go away.
        go off
        go home
        leave

55

draw out (iii)

A. She's very nice, of course, but she's terribly, terribly shy.
B. Oh, don't worry – Mrs Burke will make her talk. Mrs Burke has a genius for drawing people out.
A. Well, if she can draw Pat out, she really is a genius.

(b) **Mrs Burke** has a **genius** for drawing **people** out.
                  gift   folk
                  flair

(a) Well, if she can draw **Pat** out, she really is a genius.

draw up (i)

A. I was standing looking across the road, when all of a sudden a car drew up, and as it drew up, two men jumped out and pushed me into the back seat.
B. And then what happened?
A. They looked at my face – and then they pushed me out again.

(a) **All of a sudden**, a car drew up.
   Suddenly   taxi
   All at once   lorry
                 van
                 vehicle

(b) **Then what happened**?
   What happened then
                 next
                 after that

draw up (ii)

A. My solicitor's drawn up the agreement, and I hope you won't mind paying half of the agreement fee.
B. I'm afraid the fee for drawing that up is entirely your responsibility.
A. But, surely, it's the usual practice to share the costs.
B. Perhaps it is usual. But this is a rather unusual agreement, isn't it?

(a) My solicitor's drawn (up) the **agreement** (up).
        contract
        lease
        will

(b) I'm afraid the **fee for** drawing that up is **entirely your** responsibility.
    cost of   altogether
          not my

draw up (iii)

A. I've drawn up my soldiers on this side. You must draw yours up on that side. Then, when they're ready to fight, I'll give the signal.
B. No, I'll give the signal.
A. I'll give the signal.
B. Well, if that's the way you feel, I'm not going to draw my soldiers up at all – I'm going to put them all back in the box.

(a) I'll give the signal.
(b) Well, if that's **the way** you feel, **I'm not going** to draw (up) my **soldiers** (up)
      how   I refuse   men
            I don't intend squad
                  platoon
                  forces
                  army

at all.

dress down

A. I shall give that young fellow a real dressing down when I see him. He needs a bit of discipline!

B. What are you going to dress him down for? What's he done wrong?

A. I don't know yet. But he's sure to have done something wrong!

(a) I shall give **that young fellow** a real dressing down.

<table>
<tr><td></td><td>man</td><td>good</td></tr>
<tr><td></td><td>lad</td><td>thorough</td></tr>
</table>

    him
    John

(b) Why? What's he **done wrong**? What are you going to dress him

               been doing
               been up to

  down for?

(a) I don't know yet. But he's **sure** to have done something **wrong**!

                       certain   he shouldn't
                                                 oughtn't to

dress up (i)*

A. Did you like dressing up when you were a child?

B. Oh, yes – I used to dress up in father's old hats, and pretend to be a cowboy.

A. And I dressed up in mother's old coats, and pretended to be a queen.

B. Mm. Now that you mention it, I need a new hat.

A. Now that you mention it, I need a new coat.

(a) Did you like dressing up when you were **a child**?

                              little boy
                                      girl
                        little
                        small

(b) Oh, yes – I used to dress up in **father's old hats**.

                              mother's old coats

dress up
(ii)*

A. I really don't know how she does it! She has six children, and no help with the house, and yet by ten this morning she was dressed up in her best clothes as if she was going to a garden party or something.

B. And you've only got one child, and he's grown up, and I help you with the house, and yet at three in the afternoon you're not even out of your dressing-gown, let alone dressed up! And we are supposed to be going to a garden party!

(a) By **ten** this morning she was dressed up **in her best clothes**.

> dress
> frock
> hat
> to the nines
> to kill

(b) And you're not even out of your **dressing-gown**, let alone dressed up!

> house-coat
> overall
> working clothes

drop in

A. We've five minutes to spare. Shall we drop in at Alan's for a drink?

B. He's not expecting us.

A. Oh, he won't mind if we drop in for a moment.

B. He mightn't be at home.

A. Oh, I think he probably will.

B. He mightn't have anything to drink.

A. And he mightn't have a nose on his face!

(a) Shall we drop in at **Alan's** for a **drink**?

> nightcap
> sherry

(b) He's **not expecting** us.

> isn't

(a) He won't mind if we drop in for a **moment**.

> minute
> moment or two
> minute or two
> a bit
> a while

drop off   A. Why not relax for just half an hour? Close
your eyes. Count sheep, or something – who
knows, you might just drop off for a minute
or two.
B. All right, then. But if I do drop off, wake me
as soon as Martin arrives, won't you?
A. Don't worry – he'll be coming on that
dreadful motor-bike of his again. I don't
think I shall need to wake you up!

(a) Who knows, **you might** just drop off.
            perhaps you'll
(b) If I do drop off, wake me **as soon as** Martin arrives, won't you?
            the moment

drop out   A. I thought twenty people had entered for the
contest.
B. One's dropped out.
A. Who?
B. I'll give you one guess!
A. Why's he dropped out this time?
B. He doesn't think the standard of the others is
high enough.

(a) Why's he dropped out of the **contest** this time?
                        race
                        competition
                        hundred metres
                        hurdles
                        cross-country
(b) **I'll give you one guess**!
    Shall I give you one guess?
    Would you like me to give you one guess?

60

ease off   A. How is he today?
B. I think the pain's eased off a little. It usually
eases off in the mornings, but . . .
A. But at night it's just as bad again, I suppose.
B. Yes. He says the pain's 'rather unpleasant' at
night. And when grandfather says 'rather
unpleasant,' you càn be sure the pain's
absolutely awful.

(*a*) **How is he**   **today?**
How's Grandfather this morning
        Uncle
        John
(*b*) I think **the pain's** eased off **a little**.
        his headache's   a bit
        the spasms have   somewhat

egg on   A. He's not the real culprit, of course. I know
he's the one who actually stole the car, and
he's the one who got caught. But the real
rogue is his elder brother. The brother egged
him on. He egged him on, and told him he
wouldn't be a real man until he'd done
something really big.
B. Quite honestly, I think you're wrong. He
doesn't need anyone to egg him on. And I
don't think he deserves your sympathy, either.

(*a*) The **brother** egged him on.
        friend
        others
        rest
        family
        gang
(*b*) **Quite honestly, I think you're wrong**. He doesn't need anyone to egg him on.
        To be honest   mistaken
        Quite frankly   I don't agree with you
                        accept that
                        think that's true
                        think you're right

end up*
A. I just don't know where he'll end up!
B. Boys like him usually end up in one of two places: either at the top, or in prison.
A. And somehow, I hardly think he'll end up at the top.

(*a*) I **just   don't know** where he'll end up!
    really can't imagine
        couldn't say
   shouldn't like to say
(*b*) He'll end up **in prison**.
           gaol
        at an approved school
        at a detention centre
        as a failure
        as a success
        at the top
        in Parliament
        as a millionaire
           tycoon
           press lord
        an oil baron

enter up
A. You can total the results, and I'll enter them up in the book.
B. No, you can total them, and I'll enter them up.
A. You entered them up last time.
B. You totalled them last time.
A. We need a change.
B. We need to be consistent.
A. But you're better at adding up than I am.
B. No I'm not – I'm better at entering up than you are.
A. Shall we both do both?
B. No, let's both do neither. I'll buy you a drink.
A. No, I'll buy the drinks.

(*a*) I'll enter (up) the **results** (up).
   Let me   totals
   Shall I   amounts
             figures
             receipts
(*b*) No, I'll enter them up.

even up   A. They've caught three of our men, and we've
taken only one of theirs.
B. So you want us to even up the score?
A. Either even it up, or make it four-three to us.

(*b*) So you want **us** to even (up) the score (up)?
                 me
                 John
                 our men
(*a*) Either even it up, or make it four-three **to us**.
                                     in our favour

explain   A. It's no use trying to explain it away – the
problem exists, and you've created it.

away*   B. I'm not trying to explain it away, sir. Don't
misunderstand me. I accept there's a problem
and that I'm partly responsible for creating it.
But even so, . . .
A. You're a fool, and a failure, and you're fired!
Explain that away if you can!
B. Yes, sir. Well, in the first place, sir, I . . .

(*a*) It's no use trying to explain (away) the **problem** (away).
                                     situation
                                     crisis
                                     difficulty
                                     complaints
                                     criticisms
                                     failure
(*b*) I'm not trying to explain **it** away, **sir**.
                           them   Mr Smith

fall off
(i)*

A. In this way, our production will increase ten times. So, er, if you wouldn't mind signing now . . .

B. And the quality of the goods?

A. No one will detect any falling-off in quality. Not immediately, at any rate.

B. But the quality will fall off?

A. There will, of course, ultimately and unavoidably, be a slight deterioration in the standard of workmanship and materials, but . . .

B. I don't like the idea. I don't like it at all.

A. You don't have to like it.

B. But I do have to sign. I see.

(*b*) But the **quality** will fall off?
         standard of workmanship
                 craftsmanship
       level of accuracy
(*a*) There will, **of course**, be a slight deterioration.
       naturally
       I'll admit
         agree
       I'm forced to admit

fall off
(ii)*

A. Well, shall I deliver my lecture just to you? Or shall we both go home?

B. I can remember when at least a hundred members came to lectures such as this. And then, gradually, the numbers began to fall off.

A. You won't want me to lecture just to you, surely?

B. As I say, the attendance fell off, and for the past four lectures, only two of us have been present. But we've really enjoyed ourselves!

A. But tonight there's only you.

B. And you – two of us. Do begin, please.

(*b*) As I say, the **attendance** fell off.
               membership
               audiences
(*a*) But **tonight** there's **only** you.
       today   no one but
       this evening   nobody but

fall out

(i)

A. Squad, attention!
B. Sergeant! Private Pratt is too short to be in the Guard of Honour.
A. Private Pratt, fall out!
B. And, Sergeant, Private Higham is too tall to be in the Guard of Honour.
A. Private Higham, fall out!
B. And I'm not sure that you yourself are entirely suitable in one respect, Sergeant.
A. Sir?
B. Have you tried dieting?

(*a*) **Private Pratt** is too **short**.
    Private Higham   tall
(*b*) **Private Pratt**, fall out!

fall out

(ii)

A. By sheer luck, it fell out that you were the right man in the right place at the right time.
B. And it 'fell out' also, as you put it, that there was someone to notice that I was the right man.
A. You're very kind.
B. I've always been grateful to you.
A. That's what I came to talk to you about. I was wondering if . . .
B. But, on the other hand, I must tell you quite frankly there's no room for any more of your relatives in this organization.

(*a*) By sheer **luck** it fell out that you were **the right man**.
        good fortune   the man for the job
        chance   just what was wanted
                                            needed
(*b*) **I've always been** grateful to you.
    I shall always be

fall out
(iii)*

A. When we were children, we fell out several times a day.
B. And quickly became friends again.
A. Now, we don't fall out so often.
B. Mm. Or become friends again so quickly.

(a) When we were **children** we fell out **several times a day**.
           young   over and over again
                                        time and time again
                                        time after time
                                        all the time
                                        every other minute
(b) And **quickly** became friends again.
    soon
    very soon
    immediately
    in next to no time
    in a very short time

fall
through

A. So the scheme's fallen through!
B. Are you surprised?
A. Not really – though it was quite a good scheme, I thought.
B. Soper is full of good schemes.
A. But they all fall through.
B. I remember just one of his schemes that didn't actually fall through.
A. What was that?
B. I can't remember the details. But for some reason he withdrew it, before it had a chance to fall through.

(a) So the **scheme**'s fallen through!
    plan
    proposal
    idea
(b) **Are you surprised**?
    Does it surprise you

fed up
A. I'm fed up.'
B. Again?
A. Well, there's nothing to do here.
B. It depends on your tastes, I suppose.
A. I'm utterly fed up, both with the place, and with the people.
B. Actually, some of the people are getting just a little bit fed up with you, you know.

(a) I'm **utterly** fed up with the **place**.
   completely   people
   absolutely   food
   quite   job
                       boss
                       climate
(b) It depends on your tastes, I **suppose**.
                       reckon
                       think
                       agree
                       admit
                       should imagine
                               think

feed up
A. He's rather a bony creature, isn't he?
B. Oh, he just needs feeding up a bit – he'll soon become fat, if you feed him up a bit.
A. Feed him up? He doesn't look to have been fed at all for a very long time. I'll feed him up, all right. But why haven't you looked after him properly?
B. Well, it's a long story.
A. And I should think it's probably a tall story too!

(a) He's **rather bony**, isn't he?
    a bit   skinny
            scraggy
(b) He'll soon **become fat** if you feed him up a bit.
            fatten up
            gain weight
            put on weight

67

ferret out*
A. He's tremendously inquisitive and conscientious, and he's very tenacious. I assure you, if there are any facts to be discovered, Peake will ferret them out for us.
B. Don't you think we could ferret out a few for ourselves?
A. I'm sure we could. Yes. Yes, I should imagine we could. But it might mean missing our lunch, you know.
B. And – as you say – Peake is entirely dependable.

(*a*) **Peake** will ferret out **the facts.**
                  details
                  references
                  papers
                  documents
        what we're looking for
        what we want to know
        what we need to know
(*b*) Don't you think we could ferret out **a few for ourselves?**
                     one or two
                     two or three
                     a fact or two

fiddle about
A. Oh, do stop fiddling about! Phone a garage!
B. I'm not fiddling about – I'm trying to trace the trouble.
A. Telephone a garage. You know you don't know anything about engines. The more you fiddle about, the worse it'll be.
B. I am not fiddling about!!
A. All right, all right. You're assessing the situation.
B. Yes. Yes, that's it. And now, er ... having assessed the situation, I've decided, er ... to telephone a garage.

(*a*) Oh, **do stop fiddling about!**   **Phone a garage!**
    why are you fiddling about? Get some help
    don't fiddle about so much   assistance
(*b*) I'm not fiddling about.

68

fill in

A. What do you do most of the time?
B. Most of the time, I fill in forms.
A. What sort of forms?
B. Statistical returns, report forms, application forms – any forms.
A. The Americans don't call that filling forms in, they call it filling forms out. It's just a different way of saying the same thing, of course. Still, it might make a change for you.
B. Yes, I suppose I could tell myself for a change that I was filling them out instead of in. Though, of course, I should know very well, really, I was only filling them in, shouldn't I?

(a) **What do you do most of the time?**
How do you spend most of your time
(b) Most of the time, I fill (in) **forms** (in).
application forms
reports
orders
various details
names and addresses

fill out

A. John's filled out a bit since I last saw him.
B. Filled out? He's more than filled out – he's got fat!
A. You must be feeding him too well.
B. I feed him on salads.
A. Perhaps he doesn't get enough exercise.
B. He walks to the station every morning.
A. There are some men who always seem to fill out the moment they reach forty. Now John's forty . . .
B. And he's certainly filling out!

(a) **John's** filled out **a bit** since I last saw him.
little
somewhat
quite a lot
considerably
tremendously
(b) He's more than filled out – he's got **fat!**
stout

fill up
(i)**

A. You have to fill in the details here.
   Have you filled up a form like this before?
B. Oh, you don't need to tell me about either
   filling forms up, or filling them in – I fill
   forms in and up all day long, day in and day
   out.
A. I see.
B. But did you know the Americans call it filling
   a form out?
A. No, I didn't know. I suppose it makes a
   change, though.
B. Not really, it doesn't.

(a) You have to fill (in) the **details** (in) here.
                         answers
                         statistics
                         information
                         your name
                         address
                         date of birth
(b) Oh, **you don't need** to tell me about filling (up) forms (up).
       you've no need

fill up
(ii)*

A. What's your recipe for a good party?
B. My recipe? Mm. Yes. Yes, that's easy.
A. Let's have it, then.
B. Fill up the room, fill up the glasses – and the
   rest'll take care of itself.

(a) **What's** your **recipe** for a good party?
    Tell me   prescription
(b) That's easy.
(a) Let's have it, then.
(b) Fill (up) the room (up), and fill (up) the glasses (up).

filter out* A. They did try to suppress his report. But he was right in thinking that the facts would gradually filter out.
B. You say he showed you the report?
A. He did.
B. And after that, the facts, as you put it, 'filtered out'.
A. Yes. After that, they did.

(b) After that, the **facts**, as you put it, 'filtered out'.
           details
           proposals
           recommendations
           truth
           news
(a) **Yes**. After that, **they** did.
    That's right   it
    That's it
    That's correct
    You're quite right

**find out
(i)*** A. You'd better find out the answer by lunch time.
B. But how can I find it out?
A. How should I know? You're making the inquiry.
B. But where did it happen?
A. Find out!
B. And when did it happen?
A. You must find out!
B. And who did it?
A. Find out, Percy, find out! And if you don't find out, get out!

(a) You'd better find (out) the **answer** (out) by   **lunch time**.
                        names   this evening
                        address   tomorrow morning
                        telephone number two o'clock
                        information
(b) But how can I find it out?
(a) How should I know? You're making the inquiry.

**find out
(ii)**

A. One day I saw him stroking our cat.
B. And that was how you found him out?
A. That was how I found him out.
B. But I don't understand.
A. Well, the real Mr Corrigan was a very brave man, as we all know. But he was absolutely terrified of cats.

(a) One day I saw him **stroking our cat.**
                   writing with his left hand
                   smoking
                   watching television
(b) And that was **how** you found him out?
              the way
(a) That was **how** I found him out.
          the way

**finish
off (i)**

A. I'll show you where it is, if you like. But I must just finish off this job. It won't take more than a minute. Can you wait?
B. Oh, yes – a minute or two won't make any difference.
A. Well, actually, it might take about ten.
B. In that case, I'm afraid I really can't wait – it's rather urgent.

(a) I must just finish (off) this **job** (off). Can you wait?
                  work
                  piece of work
                  chapter
                  page
(b) **Oh, yes –**   **a minute or two** won't make any difference.
   Of course I can   a moment
   Yes, of course   one or two minutes

**finish
off (ii)**

A. He wasn't quite dead, no.
B. With three bullets in him!
A. And when they saw he was still alive, one of them picked up a spanner and . . .
B. And finished him off.
A. To put it bluntly, yes. Yes, he finished him off all right.

(*a*) One of them picked up a **spanner** and . . .

  hammer
  chopper
  cosh
  an axe
  iron bar

(*b*) And finished him off.
(*a*) Yes, he finished him off all right.

fit in*

A. But surely Marriot's new plan fits in with your suggestion?
B. Oh, yes – his plan fits in reasonably well.
A. So why not accept it?
B. It's him.
A. Him?
B. His plan fits all right, but he doesn't fit in here at all. You know that as well as I do.

(*a*) But surely his **plan** fits in with your **suggestion**?

  scheme   requirements
  proposal specification
  idea
  design

(*b*) His plan fits **all right**, but he doesn't fit in here.

  very well
  quite well
  reasonably well

fit out

A. No, we don't build boats, we fit them out —
with everything from cookers to deck chairs.
B. What ships are you fitting out at the moment?
A. Oh, several big ones. And we're also fitting
out a rather nice private yacht. It belongs to
a film star.
B. Which film star?
A. I'll give you one guess.

(a) We don't build **boats**, we fit them out.
         yachts
         ships
         liners
(b) What **ships** are you fitting out **at the moment**?
    boats   at present
    yachts   just now

fix up
(i)

A. I thought you said you were going to fix up a
shelf for my books.
B. I did fix one up for you.
A. Yes, but it fell down ages ago.
B. What happened to it?
A. We chopped it up for firewood.
B. Well, then.
A. Well what?
B. How can I fix it up again?

(a) I thought you said you were going to fix (up) a **shelf** (up).
                                                  hook
                                                  notice-board
                                                  picture-rail
(b) I did fix one up.

74

fix up

(ii)

A. I think we should fix up a meeting without delay.

B. Should we have it here, or at Headquarters?

A. At Headquarters, I think. Who shall we ask to fix up all the arrangements?

B. If you want a short, business-like meeting, ask Jacks to fix it up. If you want a more leisurely affair, ask Bonham.

(*a*) Who shall we ask to fix up the **arrangements**?
> accommodation
> programme
> meals
> meeting
> conference

(*b*) Ask **Jacks** to fix **it** up.
> them

follow up

(i)

A. He's not a bad player, I agree. But somehow he seems to me to lack the killer instinct. And in my view, the killer instinct is essential in this class of tennis.

B. He's well ahead now, though.

A. Yes, but I bet he won't follow up his advantage. He won't follow up his lead. There! What did I tell you? You see what I mean?

(*a*) He won't follow up his **advantage**.
> lead

(*b*) He's well **ahead** now, **though**.
> in front   however
> even so

(*a*) There! **What did I tell you**?
> What did I say
> Wasn't I right
> You see what I mean

follow up

(ii)

A. I've just had a report from an anonymous caller. It's probably a hoax, but you'd better follow it up.

B. My feet are killing me! This'll be the sixth lead I've followed up today, and every one so far's been a false one.

A. Perhaps this'll be the real thing.

B. Want to bet on it? A pound?

A. No, thank you.

(a) You'd better follow (up) this **report** (up).
        story
        lead
        clue

(b) This'll be the **sixth report** I've followed up **today**.
       lead   this morning
              since yesterday

get about

(i)

A. Quite naturally, he thought the end of the world had come. But then, gradually, he began to recover his spirits. And with great determination he taught himself to use his artificial limbs.

B. So now he manages to get about reasonably well.

A. Yes. He can't go very far, of course. But soon he's getting an invalid car, and when he can drive that, he'll be able to get about all over the place.

(a) With **great**   **determination.** he taught himself to use his artificial
  tremendous courage
        patience
        perseverence
 limbs.
 leg

(b) So now **he manages to** get about **reasonably well**.
       can   quite well
     he's able to   fairly well
           a bit
           a little
           from time to time
           now and again
           all over the place
           just as he likes
           wherever he likes

get about (ii)

A. The family were very popular in the neighbourhood. But then, suddenly, the story got about that the husband had been in prison at some time or other.
B. It's amazing how these fantastic stories do get about, isn't it?
A. Isn't it? No one knows if the rumour was true, of course. But they left the district shortly afterwards.
B. Why had he been in prison, do you think?

(a) The **story** got about that **he'd been in prison**.

tale	gaol
rumour	he was a criminal
idea	crook
	they weren't married
	they were in debt

(b) It's **amazing** how these **stories** do get about!

incredible	rumours
surprising	

get ahead

A. If he wants to get ahead of the others, he'd better accept the new assignment.
B. Perhaps he's no ambition. Perhaps he doesn't want to get ahead.
A. He's got talent. He ought to want to get ahead.
B. He's got a family. He ought to think of them.
A. They ought to think of him.
B. Who are you thinking of? Him? Or yourself?

(a) If he wants to get ahead, he'd better **accept the new assignment**.

> post
> position
> job
> commission
> be more ambitious
> push harder

(b) Perhaps **he doesn't want** to get ahead.
he's no wish

get on
(i)

A. Grandfather still plays the odd game of tennis when he can. But, of course, he's getting on a bit now, and his eyes aren't as good as they were.

B. I'm afraid we're all getting on, my dear. Not you, of course!

A. Well, I'm eighteen, you know! And, anyway, grandfather can still beat me when he really tries.

(a) He's getting on **a bit** now.
    Grandfather   in years
    John
(b) I'm afraid **we're all** getting on!
           all of us are

get on
(ii)

A. Young Tom was only the office boy when I left. He's got on well since then, hasn't he?

B. He has got on, you're right. But he still remembers his old dad, you know.

A. Did he send you those cigars?

B. No, he didn't send them – he did better than that! He brought them. Flew over specially, in his private plane!

(a) **Tom's** got on **very** well since **then**, hasn't he?
          extremely   that time
          amazingly
          incredibly
(b) He has got on, **you're right**.
          it's true
          without a doubt
          there's no doubt about it

get on

(iii)

A. You'd think they were the ideal married couple, wouldn't you?
B. But aren't they?
A. Only in public. In private, they don't get on at all.
B. Just the opposite from us! When we're in company, we always quarrel. But when we're at home on our own, like this, we get on like a house on fire, don't we?
A. Well . . .

(*a*) **They** don't get on **at all**.
    Bill and Sue   very well
                          too well
                          so well
                          particularly
                          well at all
                          at all well
(*b*) We get on like a house on fire, don't we?
(*a*) Well . . .

get on

(iv)

A. How's your husband getting on?
B. Oh, he's much better now, thank you. How's Mrs Vernon?
A. She's fine, thanks. Yes, she's getting on nicely – though she doesn't like this weather, of course.

(*b*) How's **Mrs Vernon** getting on?
    Mr Brown
(*a*) She's getting on **nicely**, thank you.
                        very well
                        quite well
                        rather well
                        very nicely
                        quite nicely

**get
through
(i)***

A. It's infuriating! I must give him the message, but I just can't get through!
B. What does the operator say?
A. She says the line's dead.
B. Well, if you can't get through, you can't get through. What's the message, anyway?
A. It's strictly confidential.
B. But you can tell me, surely?

(*a*) I must give him **the message**, but I just can't get through!
         details
         facts
         instructions
         warning
       his orders
(*b*) Well, if you can't get through, you can't get through. What's **the**
message, anyway?   are the
instructions

**get
through
(ii)**

A. It wasn't a difficult test. Did everyone get through easily?
B. I got through.
A. And Jane?
B. She got through as well. She got a hundred per cent.
A. And what about you?
B. I didn't get a hundred per cent.

(*a*) Did **everyone** get through easily?
       everybody
       you all
       all of you
(*b*) I got through.
(*a*) **And Jane?**
       What about John
(*b*) **She** got through **as well**.
       He   too

get
through
(iii)*

A. What time will you finish?
B. Oh, I still have a bit of work to do, but I think I can get through by five. And if I shouldn't manage to get through by then, I'll ring you, shall I?
A. And if you're not home by seven, I'll ring you – remember, the Maddoxes are coming this evening.
B. The Maddoxes. Oh, yes. Yes. The Maddoxes. Yes – I wouldn't want to miss the Maddoxes, would I?

(a) What time will you **finish**?
         get through
         have finished
(b) I **think** I can get through by **five**.
    reckon
    should imagine

get
through
(iv)

A. The Government ought to pass a law about it!
B. You're talking nonsense. Legislation of that sort wouldn't have a hope of getting through.
A. It might get through if you'd support it.
B. I'm afraid it wouldn't get through even with my support!

(a) The **legislation** might get through if you'd **support it**.
    law   give it your support
    bill
    act
    proposal
(b) It wouldn't have **a hope** of getting through!
                chance
                the faintest hope

get up
(i)

A. In the old days, on a crowded bus, a man would always get up and let a lady have his seat.
B. Someone offered me his seat only the other day, grandfather.
A. I'm very glad to hear it. I thought chivalry was dead. I really thought no one ...
B. But as soon as I saw him getting up, I made him sit down again. He looked to be about your age. And I'm sure he needed the seat much more than I did.

(a) A **man** would always get up **and let a lady have his seat**.
    gentleman   and offer his seat to a lady
                                   and let an older person have his seat
(b) **Someone** offered me his seat only **the other day**.
    A man   a day or two ago
    A young man   a couple of days ago
    An old man   a few days ago
    An old gentleman   one or two days ago

get up
(ii)*

A. It can't be time to get up. It's still dark!
B. I know – it's awful, isn't it? But it is time to get up.
A. I'll just have another five minutes.
B. Oh, no you won't!
A. Oh! OH! Ha! Don't tickle! No! No! No, don't pull the clothes off! Owch! Help! Stop twisting my toes! All right, all right! You win! All right, I'll get up! I'll get up!

(a) It can't be time to get up. **It's still dark**!
                          pitch dark
                          the middle of the night
                    It isn't light yet
                    It isn't morning yet
(b) I know – it's **awful**, isn't it? But it is **time to get up**.
            dreadful   getting up time
            terrible

get up
(iii)

A. That's what I call a very attractive product!
B. It's well got up, yes. But the actual thing itself is nothing special when you look at it closely.
A. I suppose you're right. With modern packaging techniques, they get everything up so well these days, don't they?
B. Yes. That would make a fine slogan, by the way.
A. What would?
B. 'Get it up well, and it'll sell'!
A. 'It'll sell if you get it up well'!

(b) It's well got up, yes.
        I agree
        you're right
        it's true

(a) They get everything up **extremely well** these days.
                      beautifully
                      most attractively

get up
(iv)

A. As you know, we always have a special dinner at the end of the conference, but this year we're hoping to get up an entertainment as well. Nothing special, of course, but . . .
B. Who's getting it up?
A. Well, I am, actually.
B. And you were hoping I might be prepared to tell a few of my stories, one or two of my jokes. Well, yes, I suppose I . . .
A. Actually, it wasn't exactly your jokes we had in mind.
B. Oh?
A. It was your wife, as a matter of fact.
B. My wife?
A. Do you think she might be willing to play the piano for us?

(a) We're hoping to get (up) **an entertainment** (up).
                            excursion
                        a pantomime
                            trip

(b) Who's getting it up?

get up
(iv)

A. Get them up!

B. But sir, they've been out on manoeuvres for days! They're worn out. They need a rest. Can't they sleep a bit longer this morning, sir?

A. Get them up, Sergeant!

B. Yes, sir.

A. And when you've got them up, you can tell them to go back to bed for an hour.

B. Yes, sir. But why bother to get them up, then, sir?

A. Because, Sergeant, if you don't wake them up to tell them they don't need to get up, they won't know we've given them the extra hour, will they?

B. No, sir.

A. Well, then – get them up!

B. Yes, sir.

(a) Get **them** up!
　　them all
　　the men
　　your squad
　　　　platoon
(b) Yes, sir.

get up
(v)

A. Did you ever study Latin?

B. I studied both Latin and French at school. And, in the exams, I did badly in French, but very well in Latin. Yet, I can still remember my French, whereas my Latin – well, I've forgotten it.

A. But you could probably get it up again if you needed it, couldn't you?

B. I don't think I could. Actually, I got it up especially for the exam, and then, I'm afraid, I forgot it completely.

A. I was the same with Chemistry.

(b) Actually, I got (up) my **Latin** (up) just for the exam.
　　　　　　　　　　　　　Maths
(a) I was the same with **Chemistry**.
　　　　　　　　　　　Biology

84

give in
(i)*   A. It's nearly four o'clock, sir. May we give in
               our books and go home?
            B. To your first question, Alice – yes, you may
               give in your books. To your second question,
               Alice – no, you may not go home.

(a) May we give (in) our **books** (in)   **sir?**
                   exercises   Miss Smith
                   compositions Mr Brown
                   essays
                   notes
                   work
(b) Yes, **Alice**, you may give **them** in.
                      it

give in
(ii)   A. I was surprised to hear you'd given in to his
           demands.
          B. I didn't exactly give in.
          A. You yielded. And you retreated.
          B. Oh no I didn't. I made a tactical withdrawal.
          A. You lost the battle.
          B. But I'll win the war.

(a) I was **surprised** to hear you'd given in.
        astonished
        alarmed
        shocked
        disappointed
        sad
        sorry
(b) I didn't exactly give in. I made a tactical withdrawal.

85

give off
A. How can you expect me to taste it when it gives off such a dreadful stench?
B. The aroma it gives off – I prefer to use the word 'aroma' – has nothing to do with the taste. Now, do please eat it.
A. No!
B. Well, then, I shall have to lock you in again.
A. Lock me in for as long as you like! But take that with you!
B. Oh, no, no, no. No – it's for you.

(a) It gives off such a dreadful stench.
                terrible   smell
                disgusting stink
                foul
                vile
                nasty
                nauseating
            an awful
(b) The 'aroma' has nothing to do with the taste.

give out (i)
A. Please, sir, is it worth giving out the books now?
B. It is worth giving them out, Alice.
A. But, sir, it's nearly four o'clock!
B. It is nearly four o'clock, Alice, yes.
A. So there's no . . .
B. Even so, please give out the books.

(a) Is it worth giving (out) the books (out) now?
                        paints   at this time
                        paper
(b) It is worth giving them out, Alice.

**give out
(ii)**

A. It gave out some rather strange noises.
Perhaps they were signals!
B. It's a very strange object. A very strange object indeed.
A. It gave out some very high pitched squeaks, and some very low pitched buzzes. There. There it goes again!
B. Shall we run away?
A. Running away is cowardly and undignified.
B. Oh. Yes. Yes, of course – you're quite right. It would be cowardly to run away.
A. No, we'll walk away – as quickly as we can!

(*a*) It gave out some rather strange **noises**.
  sounds
  squeaks
  buzzes
  rattles
  signals
(*b*) Shall we run away?
(*a*) No, we'll walk away – as quickly as we can!

**give out
(iii)**

A. First the lights gave out, then the brakes gave out, then the steering gave out, then the engine . . .
B. The engine gave out too, sir? Dear me, you were unlucky, weren't you?
A. The engine didn't merely give out, it dropped out! Now, you sold that car to me, and . . .
B. And, as a favour, a special favour, I'm willing to buy it back from you, sir.
A. Oh, well, of course, that's very . . .
B. As scrap, you understand.

(*a*) The **lights** gave out.
  brakes
  gears
  battery
  heater
  engine
(*b*) **Dear me**, you were **unlucky**, weren't you?
  Oh dear   unfortunate
  Well well

give out
(iv)

A. And that, ladies and gentlemen, is all I have to say.

B. Before you sit down, would you mind giving out these announcements? Actually they're not very important, but I think . . .

A. What did you say? Oh, yes – announcements. Yes. Yes, of course. And now, ladies and gentlemen, I must just give out some very important . . .

B. Not very important.

A. Some not very important announcements. Now, let me see, the first is about, er, . . . ah, yes, the first . . .

(b) Would you mind giving out **these announcements?**

	notices
	results
	pieces of information
this	information
	news

(a) Oh, yes – **announcements**. Yes. Yes, **of course.**

| notices | naturally |
| | I'd be glad to |

give out
(v)

A. The food, the water, the fuel – practically all our supplies have given out now!

B. Well, hope hasn't given out entirely yet, has it? They'll come today. We must try to conserve our energy, and to be patient.

A. Hm! My patience gave out a long time ago. Anyway, you know very well they won't come either today, or the next day, or the day after that. They won't come at all.

B. Here – have a drink of this. It'll make you feel better.

(a) The **food**'s given out. **Practically** all our **supplies** have given out now!

| water | Almost | stores |
| fuel | | |

(b) Well, **hope** hasn't given out **entirely** yet, has it?

| our faith | altogether |

give up
(i)

A. Give yourself up, Frank. You can't hide all the time.

B. I'm not going to give myself up.

A. The police are bound to catch you again sooner or later, anyway.

B. If they catch me, that's all right. But I'm not giving myself up. And I'm not going to hide all the time, either. They didn't find all the money when I went to prison, you know. I'll be back in about twenty minutes. And then you and I are going out to celebrate!

(a) Give yourself up, **Frank**.
(b) **I'm not giving myself up**.
I'm not going to give myself up
I refuse to give myself up
I won't give myself up

give up
(ii)

A. But doctor, if I give up cigarettes, and I give up beer, life won't be worth living.

B. If you don't give them up, you won't live anyway.

A. Have you ever tried to give up smoking, doctor?

B. It's my job to ask the questions, Mr Smith!

(a) If I give up **cigarettes**, life won't be worth living.
      smoking
      beer
      drinking
      chocolates
      eating sweets
      the habit
(b) If you don't give **them** up, you won't live anyway.
      it

give up (iii)**

A. Don't give up, Malcolm, don't give up! You can win! You can win! Keep on running! Keep going! Don't give up! Run! Run! Don't give up, Malcolm!

B. Does he know you've come all this way to support him?

A. What? Oh, no, no. No, actually, he doesn't know me at all.

B. I see.

A. Well done, Malcolm, well done! He's done it! He's done it! I told him not to give up, you see, didn't I? And he's done it! He's won! He's won!

(a) Don't give up, **Malcolm**, don't give up!
(b) Does he know you've come all **this way** to support him?
                this distance
                these miles
(a) **Actually**, he doesn't know me at all.
    As a matter of fact
    To be honest
    To tell you the truth

give up (iv)*

A. When I get married next year, I shall have to give up my job.

B. Do you want to give it up?

A. Not really.

B. Do you have to give it up?

A. Maurice wants me to.

B. I see. And is Maurice always going to have his own way?

A. For a start, he is, anyway!

(a) I shall have to give (up) my **job** (up).
                post
                position
                work
                profession
(b) Do you want to give it up?
(a) Not really.

go ahead

(i)

A. 111 2222.

B. A Mr Tony Brown is ringing from Paris, and wishes to reverse the charges. Will you accept the call?

A. Oh, yes.

B. Go ahead, Mr Brown. Mr Brown, you're through now – go ahead please, caller.

A. Tony! How are you? What's the trouble – have you run out of money? Or are you getting married, or something?

(b) Will you accept the call?

(a) **Oh, yes**:
Yes, I will
Yes, I'll accept it
Yes, I'll accept the call
Of course
Yes, yes

(b) Go ahead, please, **Mr Brown**.

go ahead

(ii)

A. How's the new building project?

B. We didn't make much progress with it during the bad weather, I'm afraid. But now, it's going ahead very well indeed, thanks. What about your survey?

A. Oh, it started very well. But now, what with one thing and another, it's hardly going ahead at all. In fact, you might say it's stopped!

(b) The **project**'s going ahead very well indeed. What about your survey?
programme
scheme
experiment
work

(a) What with one thing and another, **it's hardly** going ahead at all.
barely
scarcely
it isn't

go (on)
ahead
(iii)

A. Philip, I'd like you to go on ahead and tell the others we're coming.
B. But they know we're coming already.
A. Even so, I want you to go ahead of us and tell them.
B. But they already know!
A. Even so, I've asked you to ...
B. They all know already we're ...
A. Go and tell them!
B. Oh, all right. But ...
A. No more buts! Off you go.
B. Oh, all right.

(a) **Philip,** go on ahead and tell **the others** we're coming.
them all
all of them
everyone
everybody

(b) **But they already know!**
But they know already
But they all know already
But everyone knows already

go off
(i)

A. He's gone off?
B. He's gone off.
A. Without saying good-bye?
B. And without paying his bill.
A. He hasn't!
B. And he's gone off with one of the maids!
A. He has?
B. He has.
A. Which one?

(b) He's gone off without **saying good-bye.**
paying his bill
leaving an address
taking his belongings
luggage
cases
shoes

(a) He hasn't!
(b) He has!

**go off
(ii)**

A. Ugh! What an awful smell! What a dreadful taste! Surely this cheese has gone off?
B. Of course it hasn't gone off – it's supposed to taste like that!
A. And smell like this?
B. You're not supposed to smell at it, you're supposed to eat it!
A. No, no, please! You can have it all! Do please, please have all of it!

(a) Surely this **cheese** has gone off!
      milk
      cream
      butter
      wine
      beer
      bacon
      meat
(b) Of course it hasn't gone off!

**go off
(iii)**

A. It looks just like an alarm clock.
B. It's an exact replica of his own alarm clock.
A. What time will it go off?
B. It'll go off at the time he sets it to go off.
A. But this time, it won't exactly wake him up when it goes off, will it?
B. Not exactly, no. Or at least, I hope not!

(a) What time will the **alarm** go off?
      bomb
      cannon
(b) At the time **he** sets it to go off.
      she
      John
      Mary
      Mr Smith

go off

(iv)

A. Did you enjoy your talk with grandfather?
B. Yes. He says I'm a very good listener.
A. That's praise indeed! What did he talk about?
B. I don't know, really. He went off into a long reminiscence about how different things were when he was a boy, and I . . .
A. Ah, yes.
B. And I'm afraid I went off into a long daydream about how different things will be when I'm a man.
A. But you've both finished in time for tea – that's the main thing. Grandfather has finished, hasn't he?

(*a*) What did **grandfather** talk about?
        grandmother

(*b*) **He** went off into a long **reminiscence**.
   She   description of his boyhood
                                  her girlhood
                 account of his early life
                 talk about her past
                 criticism of the younger generation

go on

(i)

A. I need a rest now. You go on, and I'll sit on this bench until you get back.
B. I'm not going to leave you here. And, really, I'm not bothered about going on any further. I'll stay here with you.
A. I shall be perfectly all right, dear. I've got my knitting. Now do as I say.
B. But, grandmother, I don't like leaving you on your own.
A. When you come back, I shall probably have struck up a conversation with that old gentleman over there. Now off you go. And do stop fussing!

(*a*) I **need a rest** now. You go on.
   want to sit down
      to stop

(*b*) **I'm not bothered** about going on **any further**.
      worried   any more
  I don't care   to the top of the hill

94

go on

(ii)

A. I just don't believe you!

B. Even so, as time goes on, you'll begin to realize that what I say's true.

A. As time goes on, as time goes on! I don't care about time going on – I care about me, and now, and here!

B. But as time goes on, you won't really ...

A. Or, to be more exact, I care about me, and now, and somewhere else!

(a) I just don't **believe you**!
               it
               what you say
        think it's true
        think you're right

(b) As time **goes on**, you'll begin to realize **it's true**.
        goes by   I'm right

go on

(iii)

A. At first, of course, I didn't realize what was going on.

B. And it went on right under your nose!

A. But he seemed such a nice young man.

B. And you didn't notice what was going on! Just imagine!

A. I suppose you would've noticed.

B. Naturally I would.

A. But, then, you never could mind your own business, could you?

(a) I didn't **realize** what was going on.
        notice
        understand
        know
        see
        recognize

(b) And it went on right under your nose!

go on

(iv)

A. 'Then the speaker went on to explain how he'd done it, and why he'd done it.' That's what it says.

B. Is there something wrong?

A. I don't remember going on to describe why I did it.

B. Oh. Oh, I'm sorry about that. I apologize, I thought . . .

A. Nothing to worry about – don't apologize. Actually, as I, myself, haven't the slightest idea why I did it, I should very much like your reporter to tell me!

(*a*) 'Then the speaker went on to **explain** why he'd done it.'
                say
                mention
                indicate
                point out

(*b*) **Is there something wrong**?
Is there a mistake
Have we got it wrong
Have we made an error.

go on

(v)*

A. I can't go on any longer! It's too much! When you come to see me tomorrow, you'll find me gone!

B. By 'gone', Miranda, do I take it you mean 'dead'?

A. I can't go on! I shall kill myself!

B. How will you kill yourself this time?

A. I shall throw myself out of the window!

B. Would you like me to open it for you? Or do you think you might make me some coffee first? After all, there's no real hurry – is there?

(*a*) I can't go on **any longer**!   **It's too much**!
                more   I can't bear it
      for another minute   I can't stand any more
                                It's the end for me
                                This is the last straw

(*b*) How will you kill yourself this time?

grow up

(i)

A. What does Mark want to be when he grows up?
B. He wants to be a pilot.
A. And Sybil?
B. She wants to be an air-hostess.
A. And what about you?
B. I don't think I want to grow up at all.
A. Why not?
B. Well, daddy hasn't grown up, mummy says. And I want to be like daddy.

(*a*) What does **Mark** want to be when he grows up?
(*b*) He wants to be a **pilot**.
(*a*) And **Sybil**?
(*b*) She wants to be an **air-hostess**.

grow up

(ii)*

A. How did the tradition grow up?
B. Oh! It was very simple, really. You see, the Prime Minister, two hundred years ago, was very athletic. He used to run a mile every day, to keep fit. So the day he was made Prime Minister, he naturally ran a mile that morning, just the same as on every other morning.
A. And in that way, a tradition grew up.
B. In that way – I'm sorry to say – it did! And if I'm to be fit for this afternoon's ceremony, I must finish off my training programme now. Excuse me, won't you? Up, two, three, four. Up, two . . .

(*a*) How did the **tradition** grow up?
        custom
        legend
        practice
(*b*) It was **very** simple, **really**.
      quite   actually
                in fact
                as a matter of fact

hand down

A. What lovely furniture! What beautiful antiques! Which dealer did you buy it from?
B. I didn't buy it at all – it's all been handed down. This, for instance, was handed down from my mother's side of the family.
A. And this?
B. Oh, that! Yes. That ought never to have been handed down at all – it should've died with its owner. If it'd been made of china, of course . . . But I've learnt to live with it.

(*b*) This was handed down **from my mother's side**.
                                  father's
                    by my great-great-grandfather
                                  uncle
(*a*) And this?
(*b*) That **ought never to have** been handed down at all!
        shouldn't've
        oughtn't to have
        shouldn't have

hand in

A. What would you do if I handed in my resignation?
B. I should accept it. What would you do if you handed in your resignation?
A. I should hope to withdraw if before you accepted it.
B. Are you thinking of resigning?
A. There's no harm in thinking!

(*a*) What would you **do** if I handed in **my resignation**?
                      say   a letter of resignation
                      think   my notice
(*b*) **Are** you thinking of handing in **your resignation**?
    Were   a letter of resignation
                                   your notice

hand over A. I'm afraid I must ask you to hand over your
passport.
B. Anything else?
A. And this briefcase, and your money, and . . .
B. I suppose you want me to hand my gun over?
A. No – you can keep the gun.

(a) I must ask you to hand (over) your **passport** (over).
papers
documents
briefcase
wallet

(b) **Anything** else?
Nothing

**hand
round** A. Mother, he won't hand them round. When I
I got a box of chocolates for my birthday, I
handed them round, didn't I?
B. You did, Betty. And John's going to hand his
round, so that we can all have one, aren't you
John?
A. Look – he can't answer. He can't answer,
because his mouth's so stuffed with
chocolates!

(a) I handed (round) my **chocolates** (round), didn't I?
sweets
nuts
toffees
wine gums
jelly babies
chocolate raisins

(b) You did, **Betty**. And **John's** going to hand **his** round.
hers

hang about

A. Well, don't hang about – go and fetch it!
B. I'm not hanging about, I'm waiting for Peter.
A. There's no need to hang about waiting for Peter – it isn't heavy.
B. Then Peter'll be able to carry it by himself, won't he?

(a) Don't hang about!
Stop hanging about!
Why are you hanging about?
What are you hanging about for?
(b) I'm not hanging about, I'm waiting for **Peter.**

hang on

A. I'm not quite ready. Can you hang on a minute?
B. I can't wait any longer for you – I'm going.
A. Hey, hang on!
B. I'll see you at the match.
A. Hang on! I'm coming!
B. What, in your slippers?

(a) Can you hang on a minute?
            second
            for a bit
            for a minute or two
            for one or two minutes
(b) I can't wait any longer for you – I'm going.
            another second   off
                                    going off now
                                    off to the match

help out   A. We're in rather a mess, Mr Briggs. Half of
the staff are absent. Could you possibly help
us out with the packing for an hour or so?
B. You know I'm always glad to help out
whenever I can, Mrs Meredith, but I'm afraid
I can't come myself today. I can help you
out with a bit of transport if you like.
A. Oh, good. Could you send a van round, then?
B. I'm afraid you'll have to send someone to
fetch it.

(a) Could you help **us** out with the **packing**?
            me   loading
                            deliveries
                            orders
(b) I can help you out with a **bit of transport**.
                          a van
                          lorry
                          wagon

hold
back (i)   A. Poor thing! You could see how bravely she
was trying to hold back the tears.
B. But don't you think it's better to cry at a
time like that? I think holding back your
emotions doesn't help at all at those times.
A. I know. I know. Well, she held back her tears
as long as she could, and then the poor thing
wept and wept and wept.
B. And I'm sure she feels a lot better for it.

(a) She was trying to hold (back) her **tears** (back).
                                emotions
                                  feelings
(b) But don't you think it's better to cry **at a time like that**?
                                        such times
                                        such a time
                                        those times
                                        on such an occasion
                                        on such occasions

**hold
back (ii)**

A. Why should you want to interview her again?
B. Because she's holding something back.
A. I think she's been perfectly honest.
B. Oh, yes – what she's told me so far's all been true. But I want to know what she's holding back. And I want to know why she's holding it back.

(*b*) She's holding something back.
    He
    John
(*a*) I think she's been perfectly   honest.
             he   completely frank
                            truthful
(*b*) But I want to know what she's holding back.
        wish   he

**hold
back (iii)**

A. I did want to help. I only held back because . . . well, because I thought you might think me impertinent.
B. But why should I think it impertinent of you to wish to help?
A. Anyway, that's why I held back.
B. Well, next time I shall ask for your help – then you'll have no excuse for holding back, will you?

(*a*) Anyway, that's why I held back.
(*b*) Well, next time, you'll have no **excuse for holding back**.
                              reason
                              pretext

hold over*   A. I thought all of you'd discussed this dreary
affair at the last meeting, Mr Chairman.
B. We had it on the agenda, Mr Curtis,
certainly. But we had to hold this particular
item over until today's meeting. I might even
say we held it over until you were able to be
with us.
A. Well, if I'd known you were holding it over,
I wouldn't've been here today either.
B. Quite so, Mr Curtis. Now, may we begin?

(b) We had to hold this **item** over.

issue
matter
question
topic
point

(a) If I'd known you **were holding** it over, I **wouldn't've come**.

going to hold   shouldn't've
hadn't dealt with it   I'd've stayed away
                        at home

hold up
(i)*   A. You're late again, Jenkins. Are you going to
blame the weather again today? Or have you
got a new excuse?
B. Not really new, sir. It was the signals, sir.
There was something wrong with the signals.
The train was held up for nearly half an hour.
Just outside the station. The station at this
end, that is. And, er, I was on the train, sir.
And, er, that's why I was held up, sir.
A. Mm. Well, don't stand there thinking up
tomorrow's exciting episode, Jenkins. Try to
do something useful now you are here!

(a) Are you going to blame **the weather again** today? Or have you got a new

transport system
your wife
landlady
alarm clock

excuse?

(b) **The train** was held up for **nearly half an hour**.

bus   almost an hour
plane   forty minutes
My car

hold up

(ii)

A. You're late again, Jenkins. Was it the weather? Or have you got a new excuse?

B. Quite new, sir, quite new. And rather exciting, really. I came in the van today, you see, sir, and . . .

A. And the van was held up for half an . . .

B. By bandits, sir. Yes, it was held up by bandits. But how did you guess?

A. By bandits? You mean our van was held up? Some bandits actually held our van up?

B. Yes, sir.

A. But there was nothing in it – except you!

B. The van behind was very similar to ours, sir, and that had something in it, apparently. Oh, what an exciting episode!

(a) Have you got a new **excuse**?
        story
        tale
(b) **Some bandits** held (up) our **van** (up).
        robbers   car
        raiders   lorry
        crooks   wagon
        soldiers   vehicle

hold up

(iii)

A. Don't be impertinent!

B. I'm not being impertinent, and I didn't mean to laugh. But really, you can't hold him up as a model of virtue! I know him far too well. Why, he's . . .

A. I wasn't holding him up as a model of virtue or of anything else. I was only saying that you could learn something from him.

B. Oh, yes, I could learn something from him, I'm sure. But you'd regret it if I did.

(a) Don't be **impertinent**!
        rude
        impudent
(b) I'm not being **impertinent**. But really, you can't hold **him** up as a model
                                                                    her
of **virtue**!
    rectitude
    how to behave
    correctness
(a) I wasn't holding **him** up as a model.

104

hush up   A. A scandal such as this can't possibly be
hushed up.

    B. At least I think you should try to hush it up –
for all our sakes.

    A. For your sake, you mean.

(*b*) Try to hush (up) this **scandal** (up) for **all our sakes**.

affair	everybody's sake
business	everyone's
incident	the sake of everyone
accident	everybody
report	all of us
letter	us all
criticism	
decision	

(*b*) For **your** sake, you mean.
    his
    John's

iron out*   A. I do assure you, Mr Bancroft, this is only a
little, local difficulty. It can soon be ironed
out.

    B. It's neither little nor local, Carstairs. And
quite honestly, I don't think you're the man
to iron it out.

(*a*) The **difficulty** can   **soon** be ironed out.

problem	quickly
misunderstanding	very soon
disagreement	quickly
quarrel	

(*b*) **Quite honestly**, I don't think you're the **man** to iron it out.

frankly	chap
To be quite honest	fellow
frank	
To put it rather bluntly	

keep
back (i)

A. Should I tell him everything?
B. Yes, if I were you, I wouldn't keep anything back. They'll discover the truth, in time, whether you try to keep it back or not.

(a) **Should** I tell him **everything?**
      Ought I to   all I know
                        everything I know
                        all the facts
                        what I know
(b) If I were you, I wouldn't keep (back) **anything** (back).
                              a thing
                              any information
                                  details
                                  facts

keep
back (ii)

A. 'Keep back!' he said. 'Keep back! – it might explode!'
B. So what did you do?
A. Well, as you know, newspapermen don't always do as they're told. But this time I did as the man said – I kept well back.
B. And?
A. And I'm very glad I did!

(a) 'Keep back!' he **said.** 'It might **explode!'**
             shouted   go off
             cried   go up
                            blow up
(b) **So what did you do?**
      So did you?
      What happened then?
      What did you do?
      Did you take any notice?
      Did you do as he said?
(a) I kept well back. And I'm **very** glad I did.
                          extremely
                          so

keep
back (iii)

A. What kept you back?
B. Oh, something cropped up at the office.
A. Are you sure it was at the office?
B. What else could've kept me back?
A. You tell me!

(*a*) What kept **you** back?
        him
        her
        them
        John
(*b*) What could've kept **me** back?
               him
(*a*) You tell me!

keep on

A. Keep on trying, dear, keep on trying!
B. Don't keep on telling me to keep on, while
   you sit there sipping cool drinks. Why don't
   you try to repair it yourself?
A. I want you to take all the credit, dear – as I
   keep on saying.

(*a*) Keep on **trying**,   **dear**, keep on **trying**!
        pushing John   pushing
        pulling   working
        working
(*b*) Don't keep on **telling** me to keep on, while you sit there
                calling to
                shouting to
                shouting at
                ordering
                exhorting

     sipping cool drinks.
        sherry
        champagne
        orange juice
   eating ice-cream
   eating an ice

keep up

(i)

A. I feel awful this morning.

B. Have you got a cold, or something?

A. No. But the baby has. He kept us up most of the night.

B. How does he seem today?

A. Oh, I think he's a bit better, poor little thing. But I think we can expect to be kept up for one more night at least. Probably two.

(*a*) The baby kept us up **most of the night**.
                      all night
                      all night long
                      till the small hours
                      until the small hours
                      till three
                      until four o'clock in the morning

(*b*) **How does he seem today**?
    How is he today?
    Is he any better this morning?

(*a*) Oh, I think he's **a bit** better, thank you.
                 little
                 somewhat

keep up

(ii)

A. Keep up the good work, Willis.

B. We can't keep it up for much longer, sir, unless Stores Department keep up the level of supplies. I've tried to put pressure on their Manager, sir, but he . . .

A. You keep up the production, Willis, and I'll keep up the pressure on Mr Brennan for you!

B. Thank you, sir, but there's really no . . .

A. Yes, I've been wanting to have a word with Brennan for some time now – and this seems as good a time as any.

(*a*) Keep (up) the good work (up), **Willis**.

(*b*) We can't keep it up for **much longer**, sir, unless **they** keep up the
                        very long   you

    level of supplies.
    flow of raw materials
    supply of materials
    pressure on our suppliers
            Stores Department

108

**keep up
(iii)**

A. I know. I know. Even so try to keep his spirits up, if you can, won't you?

B. I'll do my very best, doctor, you know that. But it's so distressing. So distressing. It's sometimes very hard for me to keep my own spirits up, you know.

A. I know. I know.

B. But I'll try, doctor. I really will try.

(a) **Try** to keep (up) his spirits (up), won't you?
   Do your best
   You must try
   Try your best
   Do all you can
   Do everything you can
(b) I'll try, **doctor**, I really will try.
      Dr Brown

**keep up
(iv)**

A. I'm afraid that since I stopped doing full-time research I've found it very difficult to keep up – things are moving so fast in our field of study.

B. It was just the same with me. When I left the university, I promised myself I'd read all the periodicals, I'd attend all the conferences. But I have to admit I haven't really managed to keep up with recent developments either.

(a) I've found it difficult to keep up – things are moving so fast in our **field of study**.
   subject
   branch of the subject
   line
   job
(b) I **have to admit** I haven't managed to keep up with
    must admit
    must confess
    have to confess

   recent developments.
      research
   modern research
   the latest research
   the latest developments
   all the latest ideas
        articles on the subject

kick up
A. Surely there was no need for him to kick up such a fuss.
B. Wouldn't you have kicked up a fuss in his position?
A. No, I wouldn't.
B. Then you're not the man I took you for!

(a) There was no need to kick up such a **fuss**.

din
noise
row

(b) Wouldn't you have kicked up a **fuss**?

din
noise
row

(a) No, I wouldn't.

(b) **Then** you're not the **man** I took you **for!**

In that case	fellow	to be
If you mean that	woman	
	girl	

last out
(i)
A. They want me to try to play in the two remaining matches, but my leg's begun to trouble me again – I'm not quite sure I'll last out.
B. If you don't think you can last out, oughtn't you to withdraw now, so that they can replace you?
A. If I withdraw, they'll put Pickles in my place.
B. Well?
A. Once Pickles gets in, I'll never get him out again!
B. But if your leg . . .
A. Oh, no – I'm going to try and last out till the end of the season if I can.

(a) I'm not **quite** **sure** my **leg**'ll last out.

altogether	certain	arm
entirely		wrist
absolutely		

(b) If you don't think you can last out, **oughtn't you to withdraw**?

shouldn't you withdraw
step down
inform the committee
tell the captain

last out
(ii)

A. The bad weather'll be coming soon. Do you think we've enough stores to last out?
B. You've been buying in for ages. They ought to last out, surely.
A. Even so, I think I would like to buy just a few more cans of meat – to be on the safe side, you know.
B. And you would like me to drive you all the way into town, I suppose?
A. But you shall have your morning in bed next Saturday, dear, I promise.

(*a*) Do you think we have enough **stores** to last out?
     supplies
     stock
     bread
     meat
(*b*) **They ought to last out**, surely.
     It should last out

laugh off

A. It's no use trying to laugh it off, Maurice – it's a serious matter. And you're responsible.
B. I'm not trying to laugh it off, Gwenda, believe me. And I admit I'm responsible. I admit it! But I must say, you do take life seriously, don't you?
A. Well someone has to take it seriously.

(*a*) It's no use trying to laugh (off) the **matter** (off), **Maurice**.
     question
     situation
     criticism
     remark
     thing
(*b*) **I'm not** trying to laugh it off, **Gwenda**.
     I wasn't

lay down (i)

A. They've surrendered, sir.
B. Tell them to lay down their arms.
A. Lay down your arms.
B. Tell him to lay down his rifle.
A. You. Lay down your rifle.
B. Let me see that rifle, Sergeant.
A. Sir.
B. Yes. Yes, it looks rather interesting, doesn't it?

(*b*) Tell them to lay down their **arms**.
                weapons
(*a*) Lay down your **arms**.
         weapons
(*b*) Tell him to lay down his **rifle**.
              gun
(*a*) You. Lay down your **rifle**.
          gun

lay down (ii)*

A. Stop trying to lay the law down! You're not our boss, and we don't have to take orders from you!
B. Every time I try to lay down a few simple facts for you to consider, you say I'm trying to lay the law down. 'Stop trying to lay the law down!' you say. 'Stop trying to lay the law down!' Can't you think of a new slogan?

(*a*) Stop trying to lay (down) the law (down)!
(*b*) **Every time** I lay down a **few simple facts** you say I'm trying to lay the law
    Each time   simple principle
    Whenever   sensible basis for discussion
    down.

112

lay on   A. As I said earlier, it was a splendid conference,
                 Bonham, but I wonder if next time you could
                 lay on a little exhibition? don't you think an
                 exhibition would be a good idea?
              B. I think I can lay that on without much
                 difficulty, sir. And should I lay everything else
                 on more or less as before?
              A. Just as before, Bonham, yes. Including the
                 farewell dinner, of course.
              B. Of course, sir.

(a) I wonder if you could lay (on) **an exhibition** (on)?
                           a press conference
                           extra telephones
                           coffee
                           a meal
(b) I think I can lay **that** on **without much difficulty**.
              those   any trouble
                          with very little trouble

lay out   A. I suppose they could be called the Good Old
(i)*   Days, in some respects, yes. Yes, times have
                     changed!
              B. And now you have to lay out your own
                 clothes. And sometimes you even have to
                 mend them – I've seen you, when you thought
                 no one was looking!
              A. There's nothing undignified about a bit of
                 manual labour, Mabel! But, yes, it was very
                 nice to have a valet, and to have one's things
                 laid out, I agree.
              B. The fact is, you need someone to . . .
              A. Even so, I can't really see that getting
                 married would improve matters. Not at our
                 time of life, anyway.

(a) Yes, **times have changed**!
         things are not what they used to be
(b) And now you have to lay (out) your own **clothes** (out).
                                          suits
                                          things
(a) It was **nice** to have one's clothes laid out.
        good
        useful

**lay out
(ii)***

A. I hit him six times – three times on the chin, twice in the stomach, and once on the nose.
B. Hm! And then he hit you once, and laid you out!
A. Well, a punch like that would've laid anybody out – including you.
B. We're not talking about me.
A. I could lay you out easily enough!
B. We're not talking about me! No! Stop it! No! No! Ugh!

(a) I could lay you out **easily enough**.
               soon enough
               without much trouble
                          difficulty
               with no trouble at all
(b) We're not talking about me. No! Stop it! No! No! Ugh!

**lay out
(iii)**

A. As you know, I always find it unbearable to look at a dead body. Perhaps I'm a coward, but I prefer to remember people as they were. But it was different when father died.
B. Different?
A. Well, when they'd laid him out, he looked so serene. So peaceful.

(a) It was different when **father** died.
                       mother
                       grandfather
(b) **Different?**
How was it different
In what way was it different
(a) Well, when they'd laid **him** out, he looked **so serene**.
                    her   peaceful
                                    calm
                                    tranquil
                           to be at peace
                                      rest

lay out
(iv)

A. You must agree, he laid out a fortune on publicity.
B. I don't think he laid out exactly a fortune – but he did spend a great deal of money, it's true. At least, everybody knows his name now!
A. Whether his name's worth knowing is, of course, another matter.

(a) He laid out a fortune on **publicity**.
           advertising
           entertainment
           the celebrations
           his campaign
           the project
           a house
(b) He did spend a **great deal of   money, it's perfectly true.**
           lot   you're quite right
           vast amount
              sum
           hundreds of pounds

lay out
(v)

A. This really is the most beautiful house I've ever seen! And the gardens are so lovely!
B. The house has been in the family for years, of course. But I can take some credit for the gardens.
A. Did you lay them out?
B. I didn't lay them out with my own hands, of course.– I had them laid out. But they were laid out to my specification.

(a) Did you lay (out) the **gardens** (out)?
           grounds
           rose-beds
(b) I didn't lay them out with my own hands, of course. But they were

   laid out **to my specification.**
           design
      according to my specification
                   design
                   instructions
                   wishes

leak out*

A. Now let's get this quite clear in our minds, shall we? I'm prepared to say nothing about the incident to anybody . . .
B. That's more than generous of you.
A. But if the story leaks out – then, I'm afraid I shan't be able to support you.
B. Mm.
A. Do we understand each other?
B. Oh, yes, I think so. And, after all, no one knows about it except the two of us, do they? So the story can't possibly leak out. Can it?

(a) If the **story** **leaks** out, I shan't be able to **support you**.
    truth   help
    information   side with you
    what happened   take your side
    facts   leak
(b) **It** can't possibly leak out. Can **it**?
    They   they
    The truth

**let down
(i)****

A. Hey, what are you pulling the rope up for?
B. Thanks for all your help, Mick.
A. Let it down again!
B. Sorry, my friend.
A. Come on, Frank, let the rope down. This is no time for joking.
B. Nobody's joking, Mick.
A. Frank, if you don't let the rope down now, I'll . . .
B. Good-bye, old friend. And again – thanks for your help.

(a) Come on, **Frank**, let the **rope** down. This is no time for **joking**.
                              line   fooling around
                              rope-ladder   fooling about
                                                          messing about
                                                          fiddling about
                                                          fiddling around

(b) Nobody's **joking** Mick.

116

let down
(ii)*

A. Sorry to have let you down.
B. Oh, It's er . . . it's quite all right.
A. I didn't mean to let you down.
B. No, no, no. No, I'm sure you didn't. We all make mistakes.
A. I don't usually let people down, you know.
B. I'm sure you don't. I do understand, really.
A. Oh, I'm so glad.
B. But, on the other hand, you'll appreciate that I can no longer consider you for promotion.
A. Oh, but I was absolutely depending on it! I promised my wife that I . . .
B. Of course, you can blame me for having let you down, if you like.

(a) I didn't mean to let you down.
(b) I'm sure you didn't.
(a) I don't **usually** let **people** down, you know.
            often   anyone
           very often anybody
(b) I'm sure you don't.

let off
(i)*

A. Do you think he'll let me off this time?
B. Yes, he'll probably let you off with a warning. He usually lets first offenders off. What's the matter?
A. Only first offenders?
B. Usually only first offenders. Why?
A. Oh, nothing.

(a) Do you **think** he'll let me off?
        reckon might
(b) Yes, he'll **probably** let you off with a **warning**.
        most likely   caution
        very likely   small fine

let off
(ii)

A. I mustn't disturb the neighbours, I mustn't wake the baby, I mustn't scare the cat! Well, tell me, where can I let off my fireworks?
B. You can let them off at my house, if you like.
A. Oh, thanks, uncle. Thanks. That's marvellous! Did you hear that, mother? Did you hear that? You see, Uncle Bob always understands!
B. But I don't like bangers. You haven't got any that bang, have you?

(*a*) Where can I let (off) my **fireworks** (off)?
  crackers
  rockets
  thunder flashes
  roman candles
  catherine wheels
(*b*) You can let them off **at my house**, if you **like**.
      place   want
  in my garden
  on my lawn

let on

A. But grandfather knew I was coming back at six.
B. Well, if he knew, he didn't let on.
A. Perhaps he doesn't like you. Perhaps he wanted you to go away. Perhaps he didn't want you to wait for me.
B. But he said he did like me.
A. Ah, but when grandfather doesn't like someone, he never lets on.

(*a*) But **grandfather** knew I **was coming back at six**.
                            soon
          hadn't gone far
                    out
          shouldn't be away long
          wouldn't be out for long
(*b*) If **he** knew, **he** didn't let on.
      she   she

let out

(i)*

A. Let me out! Let me out!

B. I can't hear you. What did you say?

A. Let me out! I'm sorry! Please, please let me out!

B. You'll have to speak a little louder. I can't quite hear what you say.

A. LET ME OUT!

B. Oh, you want me to let you out! Why didn't you say so?

A. Just you wait till I get out of here! I'll teach you a lesson you won't forget!

B. Mm. Well, in that case, you can hardly expect me to let you out, can you?

(*a*) Let me out! Let me out!

(*b*) **I can't hear you.**   **What did you say?**
    You'll have to speak up   do
                a bit louder   are you saying
    I can't quite catch what you say

let out

(ii)*

A. I suppose I could let the dress out just a little more. But really, madam, if I may say so . . .

B. No, you may not say so, Janet. Just let the dress out. I don't require any sermons.

A. Perhaps if you stopped having sugar in your tea, madam. Or . . . perhaps if you stopped eating all those cream cakes . . .

B. The dress, Janet! Let out the dress! Say one more word, and you'll get this cream cake right in your face!

A. But madam, I was only trying to . . . Oh, madam!

B. Don't say I didn't warn you, Janet!

(*a*) I suppose I could let the **dress** out just a **little** more.
                            skirt   bit
                            coat   little bit
                            waist-band
                            seam

(*b*) Let it out, **Janet!** Don't say **another word!**
                          one more word
                          anything else

let out

(iii)

A. Come on, admit it. Who let the cat out of the bag?
B. I didn't tell them your secret! It wasn't me, Richard, I swear it!
A. Then who did let it out?
B. Perhaps it was Caroline.
A. What? Informing on your sister?
B. I only said perhaps.
A. It was you!
B. Or perhaps it was Pamela.
A. You!
B. Oh, don't, Richard! Richard, no! No, please! Please, Richard – it was only a little secret!

(a) Who let the cat out of the bag?
(b) I didn't let your secret out, **Richard**. I swear it. **Perhaps** it was **Caroline**.
                                      Possibly
                                      Probably
                                      Almost certainly

let up

(i)

A. You've worked very hard all your life, Jim. You can afford to let up a bit now.
B. But I haven't been working at full pressure for months now. If I let up any more, I shall stop altogether!
A. I'm only thinking of you, Jim.
B. Whenever you say you're only thinking of me, Bessie, I know I have to be on my guard. How much is it going to cost me this time?

(a) You **can afford to let** up a bit **now**.
       should let   from now on
       ought to let
       need to let
(b) If I let up **any** more, **Bessie**, I shall stop altogether!
       much

let up
(ii)

A. If only the pain would let up for an hour or two, then he might get a bit of sleep.
B. I don't think it will let up, mother. Not until he's had the operation. Though perhaps the injection will help.
A. And just to think – until this week, he's never had a day's illness in his life!

(*a*) If only the pain would let up for **an hour or two**, then he might be able
  a little
  bit
  while
  time
to **get a bit of sleep**.
  little rest
rest a bit
sleep for a while
go off to sleep
(*b*) I **don't think** it will let up, **mother**.
  shouldn't imagine

live down

A. What shall I do if someone finds out what I've done? I couldn't bear the scandal.
B. Well, I suppose you could either leave the district – in which case the scandal might follow you anyway – or . . .
A. Or what?
B. Or you could stay, and try to live it down.
A. I don't think I could ever live it down, do you? But it would follow me if I moved, you're quite right. Yes, it'd follow me no matter where I went. Still, let's not be pessimistic, eh? How about a drink?

(*a*) I couldn't **bear the scandal**.
  stand shame
     ignominy
(*b*) You could try to live it down.

live in*

A. I didn't know you lived in, Miss Bennett.
B. I haven't always lived in, you know. But when Mrs Aspinall died, they asked me if I'd like a room here, and, well, there was ...
A. Do you like living on the job?
B. I love the job. But it would be nice to get away sometimes.
A. What about this evening?
B. What about this evening?

(a) **I didn't know** you lived in.
    wasn't aware
No one told me
I wasn't told
You never mentioned
(b) I haven't always lived in, you **know.**
                    understand

**lock up
(i)***

A. Don't forget to lock up, Miss Bennett, will you?
B. I never do forget, Mr Dykes.
A. Ugh! What a dreadful night! You are lucky to be living in.
B. I sometimes think so, Mr Dykes.
A. Only sometimes, Miss Bennett?
B. Well, I'll go and lock up, Mr Dykes. Goodnight.
A. Goodnight, Miss Bennett.

(a) **Don't**   **forget** to lock up, **will you,** Miss **Bennett?**

You won't			Compton
You'll	remember	won't	Dobson
			Evans
			Forbes
			Granger
			Harrison
			Ibbotson
			Johnson
			Kendall

(b) I **never do forget,**   Mr **Dykes.**

always do remember	Emmott
	Firth
	Goss
	Harlow
	Ireland
	Jackson

122

lock up (ii)

A. That man ought to be locked up! He should be locked up!
B. Now, Mrs Thomas, remember it's Christmas – the season of goodwill. Try to be a little more charitable.
A. Locked up, that's what he should be – locked up!
B. It's Christmas, Mrs Thomas.
A. Well, then, he ought to be locked up the moment Christmas is over!

(a) That **man**   **ought to be locked up**!
         chap   should be
         fellow
         rogue   needs locking
         villain

(b) Try to be a little more **charitable, Mrs Thomas.**
                           kindly
                           generous
                           forgiving
                           magnanimous

lock up (iii)

A. And you say you locked them up in the safe before you went home?
B. That's right, officer. I locked them all up.
A. And the safe was still locked this morning?
B. That's right, officer. But as I said, the jewels were gone.
A. And your partner hasn't come yet today?
B. That's right, officer.

(a) And you say you locked (up) the **jewels** (up) in the safe?
                                    necklace
                                    bracelet
                                    rings
                                    ear-rings
                                    diamonds
                                    rubies
                                    money
                                    cash
                                    banknotes

(b) That's **right,**   **officer.**
          correct   Sergeant
                        Inspector

look
ahead*

A. The old man's left you a fine business!
B. Well, yes and no. Certainly the order books are full, and our labour relations are as good as they are anywhere. My only regret is that father couldn't, or wouldn't, look ahead a bit more.
A. Look ahead to what?
B. Oh, to new techniques, new markets, new materials.
A. Even so, he did leave you in charge of the business rather than Michael, didn't he? Wasn't that looking ahead?
B. Yes. Yes, I suppose it was.
A. I know your father thought it was, anyway.

(b) Father **wouldn't** look ahead.
        didn't
        failed to
(a) Look ahead to what?
(b) Oh, to new **markets**.
       techniques
       materials

look over*

A. Sometimes it's very nice having a lawyer in the family!
B. You mean you've decided to buy the house, and you want me to look over the contract for you before you sign it.
A. That's if you can spare the time.
B. I think, if you don't mind, I'd like to look the house itself over first.
A. Well, father, as you know, I've already . . .
B. Not that I don't trust your judgement, of course.
A. Of course.

(b) You want me to look (over) the **contract** (over) for you?
                      agreement
                      plans
(a) That's if **you can spare the time**.
        afford
      you're not too busy
(b) I'd like to look the **house** itself over first.
             flat

124

look up
(i)

A. It isn't often we hear you humming to yourself at this time in the morning, Alan. Things must be looking up for you.

B. Things are looking up. Business is looking up, my shares are looking up – and even the weather's looking up. How's life with you, by the way?

A. Well, as you say, the weather's looking up!

(a) Things must be looking up for you.
(b) **Business is** looking up. Even the weather's looking up.
   The market's
   Trade's
   My shares are
   The international situation's

look up
(ii)

A. Please, Mr Jarvis, what does this word mean?

B. Look it up in your dictionary, boy. That's what the dictionary's for.

A. Yes, sir. But I've already looked up the word I couldn't understand originally, sir, and the dictionary says it means this word. This word here, sir.

B. Let me see. Ah. Well, now you must look that word up, mustn't you?

A. I have done, sir. But, as you can see here, sir, it means the same as the word I was looking up in the first place.

(a) Please, **Mr Jarvis**, what does **this word** mean?
   'epitome'
   'mendacious'
   'acme'
   'terrestrial'
   'vindicate'
   'abrasive'
   'obtuse'

(b) Look it up in your dictionary, **boy**.　　**That's what the dictionary's for**.
   　　　　　　　　　　　　　　　girl　　That's why you have a dictionary
   　　　　　　　　　　　　　　　John

look up
(iii)

A. There's the announcement. Well, good-bye, Bill. Thanks for everything. Don't forget to look us up if ever they send you to our country, will you?

B. Thanks. I'll certainly look you up if ever they do. But I can't say when they will, or even if they will.

A. Still, you never know.

B. Actually, you know, they're sending Mr Burnhill out to your country next month. Perhaps you wouldn't mind if I told him to look you ...

A. Burnhill? Wait a minute. Isn't he the man who ...

B. Er, no. No, perhaps not. I won't say anything to Burnhill, eh?

A. Good-bye, Bill.

B. Good-bye. Safe journey. Remember me to your wife!

(a) **Don't forget** to look us up if ever they send you to our **country**, will you?
    Remember   part of the world
(b) Thanks. I'll certainly look you up if ever they do.

make
out (i)

A. He tried to make out that he hadn't been back to the house.

B. And when you told him he'd been seen there?

A. He tried to make out he'd gone back for his tool-bag.

B. And when you told him he'd been seen taking the gold chain?

A. He tried to make out he'd only borrowed it.

B. Borrowed it?

A. To wear at a fancy dress ball.

B. And where is it now?

A. He's trying to make out that someone's stolen it from him.

(b) Where is the **gold chain** now?
             necklace
(a) He's **trying to make out** that someone's **stolen it**.
    makes out   borrowed
       making out   bringing it back

126

make out (ii)

A. I just can't make the fellow out.
B. He is a bit unpredictable, I agree.
A. Unpredictable! Hm! For days on end he's perfectly reasonable and helpful, and you think you understand both him and what he says, and then all of a sudden . . . I don't know! It's like trying to hold a handful of mercury.
B. Or a handful of water, perhaps?
A. I can't make him out. He baffles me completely . By the way, has he spoken to you about his new scheme?
B. No, he's written me a memorandum about it. But I can't for the life of me make out what it means.
A. Shall we go and ask him?
B. Or shall we go for lunch?

(*a*) I just can't make the **fellow** out.
                chap
                man
                woman
(*b*) And I can't make out what **his memorandum** means.
                her letter

make out (iii)*

A. There it is! Look! You can just make it out in the distance.
B. Where? I can't see it.
A. There. Over there. Can't you just make it out among the trees?
B. I can't see any castle.
A. Castle? Who said anything about a castle? She doesn't live in a castle! Do you mean to say you still can't see it?
B. You don't mean that little cottage, do you?

(*a*) There it is! Look! You can just make the **house** out **among the trees**.

	cottage	in the distance
	castle	over there
	tower	on the horizon
	church	through the mist

(*b*) **Where?**   **I can't see it.**
    Where are you looking   I see no cottage

127

make

out (iv)

A. How did he do on the last assignment?
B. Oh, he made out all right.
A. And how's he doing on this one?
B. Oh, he's making out quite well, really.
A. So you think his prospects are good?
B. Yes, I think he should do reasonably well. What about your trainee?
A. He's not making out at all well, I'm afraid. In fact he's doing very badly. Let's change the subject, shall we?
B. Of course – though you started it.

(a) How did he do on the last **assignment**?
               project
               job
               contract

(b) Oh, he made out all right. What about your **trainee**?
                                 assistant

(a) He's **not** making out **at all**   well, **I'm afraid**.
   isn't   very   actually
                particularly   I'm sorry to say
                all that   to tell you the truth

make

out (v)*

A. There you are, sir.
B. Should I pay cash, or will you accept a cheque?
A. Oh, a cheque will be perfectly all right, sir.
B. Who should I make it out to?
A. Would you make it out to 'Jennings and Son Ltd.' please?
B. I didn't know Mr Jennings had a son.
A. I'm sure he sometimes wishes he hadn't, sir. But on the whole he seems to find me useful to have around.

(b) Who should I make (out) the **cheque** (out) to?
                           receipt
                           invoice
                           bill

(a) Would you make it out to '**Jennings and Son Ltd.**' **please**?
                   'Jennings and Co Ltd.' if you don't mind

128

make up
(i)

A. He's not a dishonest boy, Mr Jones.
B. Oh, I'm not saying he's dishonest. No, he's just careless, that's all. Even so, a pound is a pound, and a loss is a loss.
A. Here, let me make it up out of my own pocket, Mr Jones.
B. If I were you, I'd make him make it up out of his own pocket, Mr Smith. It'll teach him not to be careless.

(b) Even so, a **pound** is a **pound**, and a loss is a loss. It'll have to be made up.
      dollar   dollar   The amount
                                     sum
(a) **Let me** make it up out of my own **pocket, Mr Jones**.
    Allow me to   funds
    You must let me
    You must allow me to

make up
(ii)

A. The story wasn't true, was it?
B. No, I'm afraid I made it up.
A. But why?
B. I thought you wouldn't understand if I told you the truth. So I made up the story about having been ill for the last six weeks.
A. But of course I understand!
B. Yes, now you do. But then you wouldn't've.

(a) The **story** wasn't true, was it?
    tale
    report
    account
(b) No, **I'm afraid** I made it up.
        sorry to say
    I regret to say
    I'm sorry to tell you
    I'm sorry to have to tell you
(a) But **why**?
    why did you make it up

make up (iii)

A. But he looked so different from Boodle. He didn't look in the least like Boodle. How could he be Boodle? Boodle had a moustache, and a smaller nose, and a bigger ... and anyway, he was much older than Boodle.

B. Make-up. He'd made himself up to look older.

A. Make-up? But surely he couldn't 've made up his face as convincingly as that? Why – you'll be saying that I'm in disguise next!

B. Well, aren't you?

(*b*) He'd made himself up to look **older**.

> younger
> darker
> fairer
> more haggard
> handsome
> ugly

(*a*) But surely he couldn't 've made (up) his **face** (up) as **convincingly** as that?

> nose   expertly
> eyes   professionally
> hands

make up (iv)*

A. I always buy my clothes ready-made.

B. Oh, I prefer to have them made by a proper tailor.

A. But tailors are so expensive!

B. Mr Ross isn't. If you buy the cloth yourself, he'll make it up for you for a very reasonable sum. And he'll make it up beautifully, believe me.

A. Is that one of his suits you're wearing now?

B. Yes, as a matter of fact, it is.

A. I see.

(*a*) But tailors are so expensive!

(*b*) Mr **Ross** isn't. He'll make (up) **a suit** (up) for you for a very reasonable

> a jacket
> some trousers
> an overcoat

sum. And he'll make it up **beautifully**, believe me.

amount   very well
price   marvellously
charge

130

make up
(v)

A. I'd like you to make up a list of all our products and their prices, Miss Flynn.

B. Is a list all you need, Mr Parsons, or would you like me to make up a proper catalogue, and have it printed? Everyone has printed catalogues these days.

A. No, Miss Flynn, a simple list will do very well – it's all we need. Just make up a simple list, thank you.

(a) I'd like you to make (up) a list (up) of all our **products** and their prices.
    want   lines
                                              books
                                              chairs
                                              dresses

(b) Would you like me to make up a proper catalogue, **Mr Parsons**?
(a) No, **Miss Flynn**. Just make up a simple list, **thank you**.
                                         please
                                       if you please
                                       if you would
                                       if you don't mind

make up
(vi)

A. They were quarrelling very fiercely yesterday, and now look at them!

B. They seem to have made it up.

A. Adults don't make up their quarrels so quickly, do they?

B. Oh, I don't know about that. Remember yesterday?

A. That wasn't a quarrel.

B. It was a quarrel.

A. It wasn't!

B. IT WAS!

A. Let's not quarrel.

(a) **They** were quarrelling **fiercely**   **yesterday**.
    The two of them   furiously a moment ago
    John and Susan   a short time ago
(b) They **seem** to have made it up.
          appear
(a) **Adults** don't make (up) **their** quarrels (up) so **quickly**, do they?
    Grown-ups   rapidly
    We   our   promptly we

make up
(vii)

A. Shall we have a game of tennis?
B. We need someone to make up a four if we're going to play doubles.
A. What about Crabtree? Crabtree might be willing to make up a four.
B. If you can't think of anyone better than Crabtree, we'll take it in turns to play singles. Or if you like, I'll play the two of you.

(*b*) We **need someone** to make up **a four**.
             somebody   seven
must have someone   eleven
             somebody   thirteen
                       fifteen
                       a team
(*a*) **Crabtree** might be willing to make up a **four**.

miss out

A. Haven't you missed out one point?
B. No, I think I've told you everything. I don't remember missing anything out.
A. Tell me about the telephone call.
B. Oh, you know about the telephone call! Yes, well, er . . . I don't really think I ought to tell you about that.
A. I think you should. I'm sure you should. I'll tell you what – if you tell me about the call, I might agree to miss out all reference to it in my report.
B. When you know who I telephoned, and what the call was about, I think you'll certainly agree to miss it out of your report.

(*a*) Haven't you missed (out) one **point** (out)?
                        item
                        piece of information
                        little thing
                        small point
(*b*) I don't **remember missing** anything out.
          recall
          think I've missed

mix up
(i)*

A. What's your recipe for a good party, Brenda?
B. Plenty to eat, plenty to drink, plenty of people – then mix them all up in a small room.
A. And if you have people of different ages?
B. Mix them up.
A. Different interests, different occupations, attitudes?
B. Mix them all up together.
A. Is there anything or anyone you wouldn't mix up?
B. The bores. Only the bores. You must put the bores together, and you must keep them together. That's the most important part of the recipe!

(b) Mix them all up in a small room, with plenty to **eat**.
                                                            drink

(a) People **of different ages?**
         with different interests
                        attitudes
                        occupations
         from different backgrounds
                        parts of the country
                        countries
(b) Mix them up.

mix up
(ii)

A. Yes, I remember the alarm bell ringing. But the rest is all mixed up in my mind. Perhaps you can help me to remember.
B. I think anyone in your position would feel a bit mixed up. No – I won't ask you anything else at all tonight.
A. But what happened to Tom? Tell me about Tom.
B. Nothing else tonight. Try to sleep.

(a) **The rest** is all mixed up in my mind.
     Everything else
(b) **Anyone** in your position would feel **a bit** mixed up.
     Anybody   little
                                          terribly
                                          an awfully
                                          more than a bit

133

mount up* A. The tour is supposed to cost only so much –
see. That's the inclusive price.

B. Yes, but the extras mount up. Drinks, trips to
the theatre, coach tours – a bit of this and a
bit of that, and before you know where you are,
the extras have mounted up so much you're
paying double the original price.

A. But it says the inclusive price!

B. Yes – inclusive of everything except extras!
And, as I say, it's the extras that mount up.

(a) **That's** the inclusive price.
Fifty pounds is
Five hundred dollars is

(b) It's the **extras**   **that mount** up.
    cost of the extras   that mounts
    bills for the extras that mount

(a) But it says inclusive **price**!
              charge
              rate

muster up A. I think I can muster up the money.

B. To beat them, you'll need more than money.
You'll have to muster up all your skill, and all
your courage, and all your . . .

A. And all my friends.

B. At least don't worry about your friends. I'll
muster them up for you!

(a) I think I can muster (up) the **money** (up).
                        cash
                        currency
                        amount required
                        pounds
                        dollars

(b) You'll have to muster up all your **skill**.
                        courage
                        endurance
                        cunning
                        experience

(a) And all my friends.

(b) I'll muster them up for you.

own up
    A. Why not admit it? Own up, and take your punishment.
    B. What would the punishment be?
    A. If you own up straight away, it shouldn't be severe. And if you did it – well, you ought to own up anyway, oughtn't you?
    B. I didn't say I did it.

(a) Own up, and take **your punishment**. If you **did it**,   you **ought to** own
            medicine   were the culprit   should
         the consequences
  up anyway.
(b) I didn't say I did it.

pack up
(i)*
    A. Shall we pack up our things and go?
    B. Well, this place is a disappointment, isn't it?
    A. You can just see the sea out of this top window – with a pair of binoculars!
    B. Even so, to call the hotel 'Sea View' is criminally misleading, I should've thought.
    A. And the room's damp, anyway. Yes, come on, let's pack up and go.
    B. What shall we tell the manager?
    A. Tell him the truth – it's time someone did!

(a) Shall we pack (up) our **things** (up) and go?
               bags
               cases
               luggage
               boxes
               belongings
(b) Well, this **place** is a disappointment, isn't it?
      hotel
      boarding house
      flat
      town
      city

pack up

(ii)**

A. Let's pack up now.

B. But if we work for a few more minutes, we can finish the job. Then, we shan't need to come back tomorrow – we shall be able to start a new job.

A. That's what I mean – let's pack it up now.

(*a*) Let's pack up now.

(*b*) But we can finish the job in **a few more minutes**.
  a minute or two
  a half hour or so
  another fifteen minutes
  very soon.
  next to no time

(*a*) **That's what I mean** – let's pack it up now.
  That's just what I'm talking about
  Exactly
  Quite

pack up

(iii)*

A. You remember I told you this morning that the engine was making some very ominous noises? Well, now it's packed up altogether.

B. Have you told Bruce it's packed up?

A. Not yet, I haven't. By the way, do you think he'll expect me to pay anything towards the repair? I know I was driving it – but it is his car, after all, isn't it?

(*a*) The **engine**'s packed up **altogether**.
  dynamo   entirely
  battery
  clutch
  starter
  hand-brake
  foot-brake

(*b*) Have you **told Bruce** it's packed up?
  let Tony know

pass away*

A. Just imagine – he'd never had a day's illness in his life. And then he passed away peacefully in his sleep like that.
B. Mm. He wouldn't know anything at all about it. When my time comes, I hope I shall pass away just like that. Yes – that's definitely the best way to go.
A. It'd be best for you, yes. But what about me? What about the shock?
B. Oh, it's going to be 'Gentlemen First' on that occasion, is it?

(a) **He** passed away peacefully **in his sleep**.
    Mrs Kay   her
                               during the night
                               without any pain
                               without knowing anything about it
(b) That's how I should like to **pass away**, when my time comes.
                                   pass on

pass out (i)*

A. If possible, I'd like to see your training programme in action.
B. Well, of course, this batch will be passing out next week. Then we shall be starting a new programme, and you'll be able to observe that course right from the start. But you will come to our passing-out parade next week, won't you?
A. Thank you. Actually, I already have an invitation – I'm Middleton's uncle, you know.
B. You're Middleton's uncle? Oh, I see. Yes. Yes, I, er ... I didn't know you were Middleton's uncle. Well, I, er ... I'll see you at the passing-out parade, then.

(b) This **batch** will be passing out **next week**. You will come to the passing-
    section   Thursday
    class   very soon
    contingent   in a month
  out parade, won't you?

(a) Actually, **I already have an invitation**.
         I've already been invited
         someone's already invited me

pass
out (ii)*

A. Did he win?
B. Well, of course he won. It was very dramatic, really.
A. Go on, tell me what happened.
B. Well, he just managed to cross the line before Smith. Everybody went wild. John looked very happy. And the Chairman was just going to present him with his medal when, all of a sudden, he passed out – passed out completely!
A. The Chairman passed out?
B. No, John did, you fool!

(a) The **Chairman** passed out?
        President
        Mayor
    `   Minister
        Principal
(b) No, **John** passed out, **you fool**!
                          silly
                            idiot
                    idiot
                    silly
                    stupid

patch
up (i)

A. It's time those two patched up their quarrel.
B. It's their quarrel, though, sir, surely.
A. Yes, but it's my time they're wasting.
   Tell them to patch it up, and be friends by lunch time at the latest!
B. I'll tell them.
A. Tell them to get it patched up, or they'll both have a quarrel on their hands with me – and today I feel just in the mood for a quarrel!
B. Yes, Mr Strong.

(a) It's **time**   **those two** patched up their quarrel.
       high time   the two of them
       about time   Tom and Dick
                      Fay and May
                      Billy and Lilly
                      Roy and Joy
(b) It's their quarrel, though, **sir**, surely.
                      Mr Strong

138

patch up (ii)

A. Those are the facts, Mr Winstanley. Now you must decide – do we buy a completely new machine, or do we try to patch this one up?

B. How long will it last if we patch it up?

A. It might not last very long, actually.

B. How much will it cost to patch up?

A. A quarter as much as to buy a new one.

B. Mm. I don't really like patch-up jobs. Get a new one.

A. Should I tell Mr Mercer? I suppose you'll want his opinion.

B. He's away this week, as it happens. And I don't know where I can contact him – do I, Jack? If you see what I mean.

(b) How long will the **machine** last if we patch it up?
        engine
        unit
        installation
        boiler
        lathe
        car
        motor

(a) It might not last very long, **actually**.
              in fact
              as a matter of fact

pay up

A. I know you don't like him. But you do owe him money. I think you ought to pay up.

B. But if I pay up, he'll think I'm admitting I'm wrong in the other matter.

A. Well, who cares what he thinks?

B. No, I'm not going to pay up – it's a matter of principle.

A. It certainly is a matter of principle!

(a) I think you **ought to** pay up.
        should
        must

(b) I'**m not going to** pay up – it's a matter of principle.
   refuse to
   won't

(a) **It certainly is** a matter of principle!
   It is indeed

139

pick out

(i)

A. There, madam – six pounds, you said.

B. Yes, George. But would you mind picking out the bad ones? Bad potatoes are no good to me.

A. They're no good to us, either, Mrs Collins.

B. But you bought them – you must've bought them.

A. They were sold to us, Mrs Collins. We get them by the sack, you know.

B. Well, they're not going to be sold to me. Pick them all out, George, if you don't mind.

(b) Would you mind picking (out) the bad **potatoes** (out)?

apples
oranges
plums
peas
beans
ones

They're no good to me, **George**.

(a) They're no good to us, either, **Mrs Collins**.

me

pick out

(ii)

A. Is he good-looking?

B. Yes, he's quite good-looking – but in a rather ordinary sort of way. You couldn't really pick his face out in a crowd, if you see what I mean. What about Michael?

A. Oh, he isn't a bit good-looking, I'm afraid. But, at least, with his bald head, you can pick him out anywhere!

(b) You **couldn't** pick **his face** out in a crowd. What about **Michael**?

wouldn't   him

(a) With his **bald head** you could pick him out anywhere!

big nose
long neck
funny ears
red hair

pick up
(i)

A. Left, right. Left, right. Left, right. Left, right. Pick 'em up, there! Pick 'em up! Pick 'em up, pick 'em up, pick 'em up, pick 'em up. What are you stopping for, Private Mills?

B. Excuse me, sergeant. But as you know, I'm a new recruit, and I was wondering if you'd mind telling me exactly what it is we're supposed to be picking up.

A. Feet, Private Mills, feet! Those great, big, clumsy, horrible feet in those beautiful new unpolished boots that you're going to spend this evening and the next and the next polishing and polishing, aren't you, Private Mills?

B. Thank you, sergeant.

A. Pick 'em up there! Left, right. Left, right. Pick 'em up!

(*a*) Pick 'em up there!
(*b*) What are we supposed to **be picking** up, sergeant?
                              pick
(*a*) Feet, Private **Mills**, feet!

pick up
(ii)*

A. Ruth says it's a lovely party and she wants to know if she can stay till midnight.

B. Yes, tell her she can stay, if she wants to.

A. The last bus'll be gone by that time. Shall I tell her you'll drive over and pick her up in the car?

B. Yes – tell her I'll pick her up in an hour.

A. Yes, darling – Daddy says you can stay, as it's such a lovely party. He'll pick you up just after midnight.

B. Just before midnight.

A. That's it, darling – just after midnight.

(*a*) Shall I tell **her** you'll pick her up in the car?
                Ruth
(*b*) Yes – tell her I'll pick her up **in an hour**.
                                 just before midnight
                                 after
                                 at about five to twelve
                                      past twelve

pick up (iii)*

A. What an interesting flower pot! Did you pick it up cheap at a sale?

B. No I did not pick it up at a sale. I didn't pick it up at all, I made it. And it isn't a flower pot, it's a hat!

A. You could've fooled me!

(a) What **an interesting**   **flower pot!** Did you pick it up cheap at
     intriguing   bowl
   a fascinating   lamp shade
     marvellous
     splendid
     preposterous
  an odd
     incredible

   a sale?
     jumble sale
   second-hand shop
          dealer's
  an auction

(b) No I did not pick it up at a **sale**, I made it!

pick up (iv)*

A. I can't really claim to speak the language like a native, you know, but I did pick up a bit of it while I was working there.

B. Is it easy to pick up?

A. Well, I'm one of those people who pick things up very quickly, you know. You mightn't find it so easy, of course.

(a) I did pick (up) a **bit** of the language (up).
           smattering
           working knowledge
           reasonable knowledge
           fair amount

(b) Is it **easy** to pick up?
     simple
     fairly easy
         simple

(a) You mightn't find it so **easy,**   **of course.**
             simple actually

pick up
(v)

A. Oh, I think he's picking up a bit, thank you, Mr Williams.
B. You know, your grandfather has remarkable powers of recovery.
A. I'm sure that this time he'll be all right. But last time – I must confess – I wondered whether he ever would pick up. He even said he was tired of living.
B. I see.
A. But then we discovered it was actually auntie he was tired of – and as soon as she left, he picked up quite quickly!

(a) I think he's picking up a bit, thank you.
          Grandfather
          Uncle
          my brother
          father
(b) You know, your **grandfather** has **remarkable powers of recovery**.
                            an incredible constitution
                            a very strong will to live

pick up
(vi)

A. We managed to pick up the survivors.
B. Where are they?
A. In this cabin.
B. What, all of them?
A. Yes.
B. How many did you pick up, then?
A. There were only two.

(a) We **managed** to pick (up) the survivors (up).
      were able
(b) How many did you pick up?
(a) There were only **two**.

pick up (vii)

A. How did you manage to pick up that piece of information?
B. Oh, I have my ways, you know.
A. But where did you pick it up?
B. Oh, from my usual place, you know.
A. Who did you pick it up from?
B. Oh, from my usual informant, you know.
A. How much did you have to pay him for it?
B. Oh, the amount I usually pay, you know.

(a) Where did you pick (up) that **piece of information** (up)?
        evidence
        news
        story
        idea
(b) Oh, from my usual **place**, you know.
        source
        informant

play down*

A. It is a serious crisis, yes. I know it's serious, and you know it's serious. But all the same, I want you to play it down for the next two days at least. And I want the Press to play it down, too.
B. But the public will demand an inquiry!
A. Not if you play it down for a couple of days as I've told you to do. You see the day after tomorrow, something new's going to happen. And when it does, I assure you it'll make the public forget all about this little crisis. Now do as I say.

(a) I want **you** to play (down) this **crisis** (down).
    the Press   affair
    the editor   incident
    Public Relations
(b) But **the public** will demand an **inquiry**!
      people   explanation
    people
      Government

pluck up*   A. Well, as you know, Jenny, I'm not a brave
woman, but I thought, 'Well,' I thought,
'this young man has no right to be in my
house, and he has no right to steal my things.'
   B. So what did you do, grandmother?
   A. I plucked up all my courage and . . . and I
hit him with the poker.
   B. You hit him? You really did? Oh! But how
marvellous! I should just've screamed. And
as for plucking up courage and hitting him
with a poker, well!
   A. Oh, I'm sure it's what anybody would've done
in my position.
   B. Where is he now, by the way? Did the
police arrest him?
   A. I've locked him in the cupboard until the
police come.

(a) I plucked (up) all my courage (up) and hit him with a **poker**.
                                                              vase
                                                              milk bottle
                                                              candle-stick
(b) You hit him? You really did? But how **marvellous**!
                                                wonderful
                                                splendid

pop in   A. Did Molly stay long?
   B. No, she just popped in for a moment – as
usual.
   A. To borrow something – as usual?
   B. Some sugar, actually.
   A. Well, next time she pops in to borrow either
sugar or anything else, tell her to pop out
again and buy some.

(a) Did **Molly** stay long?
(b) She just popped in for a **moment**.
                            minute
                            moment or two
                            minute or two
(a) To borrow something?
(b) **Some sugar**.
      flour
An egg
My rolling pin

145

pull
through

A. His breathing's more steady, and his pulse is regular now, Mrs Mitchell. You don't need to worry any more. He's going to pull through all right.

B. But doctor, look at him! He seems so terribly ill!

A. He is terribly ill, Mrs Mitchell. And he's going to continue to be ill for a week or two yet. But if I say he's going to pull through, he's going to pull through. So tonight, I want you to sleep at home. You can come back here first thing in the morning. But tonight, you must have a good rest. And before you go to bed, I'd like you to take this with a glass of water.

(*a*) He's going to pull through, **Mrs Mitchell**.
(*b*) But doctor, look at **him**! He seems so **terribly ill**!
                                dreadfully sick
(*a*) **Mrs Mitchell**, if I say he's going to pull through, **he's** going to pull through.

pull up
(i)

A. As I said, Dick, I really can't stay more than a few minutes, but ...

B. You've been saying that, and standing there for the last five minutes. Now why don't you pull up a chair and tell me exactly what's on your mind. You have got something on your mind, haven't you?

A. You're perfectly right, Dick. Yes, I have got something on my mind.

B. Well, then, pull up a chair, man, and sit down.

A. All right. Er ... you're not going to like what I have to say, Dick. But here goes.

(*b*) Why don't you pull (up) a chair (up)?
(*a*) Yes, I have got something **on my mind**.
                         worrying me
                         bothering me
(*b*) Well, then, pull up a chair and **sit down**.
                         tell me all about it
                         tell me what it is

pull up
(ii)*

A. It was very good of you to give me a lift.
Now, if you wouldn't mind pulling up by that
bus stop, I can easily . . .

B. What bus stop?

A. That one. That one by the post office. If you
pull up there, that'll do fine.

B. . . . What post office, Mr Bartle?

A. Bartle? Mr Bartle? I don't know anyone
called Bartle – my name's . . . Now if you'll
just pull up there, please, I'll . . .

B. Now, Mr, er . . . Would you like me to, er . . .
Is there anywhere you'd like me to drop you?

(a) If you'll just pull up by that bus stop,

> telephone box
> > kiosk
> > post office
> > tobacconist's
> > the Town Hall
> > the clock
> > the park gates

(b) What bus stop, Mr Bartle?
> post office

pull up
(iii)

A. John's asked me to be the spokesman, but
I'm quite sure that if I miss anything out, . . .

B. Or put anything in!

A. Or put anything in that shouldn't be there, . . .

B. I'll pull you up!

A. As my colleague says, he'll pull me up. Come
to think of it, he's pulled me up twice already,
and I haven't even begun! Perhaps he'd
better be spokesman.

(a) If I miss   anything out, . . .
> leave
> omit   anything
> forget to mention anything
> omit   to mention anything

(b) I'll pull you up!

(a) As he says,   he'll pull me up.
> she   she'll
> my colleague
> partner

put
across

A. Both of them are good candidates in their own way. Bray knows a great deal, but ...
B. Yes, but can he put it across to other people?
A. And Bridges can put things across very well, but ...
B. Yes, but how much does he know?
A. It is a dilemma, isn't it?
B. I think we ought to interview them again before making a decision. It has to be one or the other.
A. But after lunch, don't you think?

(a) **Bray** knows **a great deal**.
      a lot
      plenty
(b) Yes, but can he put it across to   **other people**?
      what he knows others
      his subject   the layman
      his ideas
      his points
      his knowledge
(a) And **Bridges** can put things across.

put off
(i)*

A. Don't forget to put the lights off, dear, will you? I'm going to bed.
B. Do you know, you say that every night? 'Don't forget to put the lights off, dear,' you say. Every night, you say it! It's every single night! Do you know that?
A. But if I didn't say it, dear, you wouldn't do it.
B. Well, I'll tell you this: the next time you say it, I shall refuse to do it!
A. Of course, dear, of course. I know exactly how you feel. I quite understand your feelings. But you will remember, won't you? To put them off, that is?

(a) Don't forget to put (off) **the lights** (off).
        light
        dining-room light
        sitting-room
(b) Do you know, you say that every night! Every night you say it! It's every single night!

148

put off
(ii)*

A. I don't want to put you off the house, of course.
B. But you say the woodwork is rotten?
A. Well, yes, it is a bit rotten.
B. And the roof leaks?
A. It does leak a bit, yes.
B. And the tree outside the window creaks all night?
A. Only when there's a wind, you know.
B. And you really did see a rat in the kitchen?
A. As I say, I don't want to put you off. I shouldn't want to put you off the house, at all. Actually, it was two rats.
B. Two?
A. At least two, yes.

(a) I don't want to put you off the house.
　　　　　　　　　　　　　cottage
　　　　　　　　　　　　　buying the house
(b) But you say the woodwork is rotten?
　　　　　　　　　　roof leaks
　　　　　　　　　　tree creaks
(a) As I say, I don't want to put you off it.

put off
(iii)

A. What time did their boat put off?
B. Oh, they put off at about midnight, sir.
A. And did you check their papers?
B. Why should I check their papers, sir?
A. You let them put off without checking their papers?
B. They said they'd be back just after dawn, sir.
A. It's after dawn now, man, it's after dawn now!
B. Yes, sir. And they've come back. Actually they've brought me a nice big fish, sir. Would you like to share it?

(a) What time did their boat put off?
　　　　　　　　　it
(b) Oh, they put off at about midnight, sir.
　　　　　it　　　　　　　　ten o'clock
　　　　　　　　　　　　　just before eleven
　　　　　　　　　　　　　after

149

put off
(iv)*

A. I'm terribly sorry, Mr Graham. Didn't you know the meeting's been put off till next week?
B. I did not know, Miss Kendall! And if the meeting's been put off, I want to know why I wasn't told!
A. Somebody's made a mistake, I'm afraid.
B. And someone's going to suffer for it, I'm afraid!

(a) **Didn't you know** the meeting's been put off, **Mr Graham**?
    Did no one tell you
    Didn't anyone tell you
    Did nobody let you know
    Weren't you told
(b) **I did not know** it's been put off, **Miss Kendall**!
    No one did tell me
            let me know
    I wasn't told

put off
(v)*

A. Mr Pratt to see you, sir.
B. Sally, I thought I told you to put him off!
A. I tried to put him off, Mr Barrington, but I couldn't contact him.
B. Oh, all right. Send him in. Why couldn't she have put the fellow off? He's a fool and he's a nuisance, and what's more, he's a ... Ah, Mr Pratt! How are you? Do sit down. I'm so glad you were able to come.

(a) **Mr Pratt** to see you, sir.
(b) **Sally**, I thought I told you to put **Mr Pratt** off!
                            him
                            her
                            the fellow
                            the woman
(a) I tried to put **him** off, sir, but **I couldn't contact him**.
            her   find   her
                    he wasn't available
                    she's not on the telephone

put off
(vi)

A. Nicholas isn't as bad as all that.
B. Oh, he's perfectly all right except that he will do such childish things!
A. Yes. Yes, he'll certainly have to put off some of his boyish ways when he goes to college.
B. What makes you think college will help him to put them off?
A. Henry, you're getting bitter. And you're getting old.

(a) **Nicholas** isn't as bad as all that.
(b) But **he** will do such childish things!
      she
(a) Yes, **he**'ll have to put off some of **his boyish ways**
      she   her girlish
                                 youthful habits
                                 childish tricks

when **he**   **goes to college.**
      she   the university
         starts work
         starts his new job
              her

put over*

A. This policy is just what is needed, of course, but how can we put it over to the electorate? Who can put it over?
B. I know who could put it over. But I don't think he'd want to.
A. Why wouldn't he? It's a sound policy.
B. Oh, it is a sound policy, yes. But it's rather a pity he didn't think of it. Or at least, it's a pity he wasn't made to think he'd thought of it!

(a) Who can put this **policy** over to the electorate?
                     programme
                     plan
                     idea
                     scheme
(b) I know **somebody** who could put it over. But I don't think he'd want to.
      a man
      someone

**put
through
(i)***

A. Oh, I'm sorry – did I put you through to the wrong extension?
B. I'm afraid you did. You put me through to the cloakroom. It was Mr Barrington's extension I wanted.
A. Oh, I'm terribly sorry. I'll put you through now, Mr Pratt.

(a) Oh, **I'm sorry**, did I put you through to the wrong **extension**?
    so sorry   number
    terribly sorry
    extremely sorry
(b) You put me through to the **cloakroom**.
                    canteen
                    kitchen
                    porter's desk

**put
through
(ii)**

A. If he can put this plan through, he can put anything through. It isn't a very good plan.
B. But he thought of it, and he thinks it's good. And those are two very good reasons why he'll do everything in his power to put the plan through. And when he tries really hard, well, you know as well as I do, he very rarely fails.

(a) If he can put this **plan** through he can put anything through.
            scheme
            proposal
(b) He'll do everything **in his power** to put it through.
               he can
               possible
               humanly possible

put up
(i)**

A. Put the ladder up!
B. What did you say?
A. The ladder. Put it up again. Why've you taken it down?
B. If I put it up again, you'll come down it.
A. Well, that was the idea, wasn't it?
B. That was your idea, yes.

(*a*) Put the ladder up!
(*b*) **What did you say?**
What was that
I didn't catch what you said
What
Eh
(*a*) The ladder. Put it up again.

put up
(ii)

A. When are you going to sell, George?
B. When I do sell, Frank – if I sell – it won't be to you, you can be sure of that. I don't want you putting houses all over my land.
A. But the houses I put up are of the highest quality, George. Surely you admit that?
B. I'm not concerned with the sort of houses you put up, Frank. I'm only concerned with where you put them up – and with where you're not going to put them up, if I can prevent it.

(*a*) When are you going to **sell,**   **George?**
               sell your land
(*b*) I don't want you putting (up) **houses** (up) all over my land.
                     flats
                     offices
                     garages
                     sheds
                     buildings
(*a*) But the houses I put up are **of.the highest quality,**   **George**.
                         standard
               built to the highest standard

put up
(iii)

A. I'm afraid he lost.
B. I don't care whether he lost or not – he couldn't expect to win. But the point is, did he put up a good fight? Did he put up a good fight, or didn't he?
A. Oh, yes, he put up a very good fight. At least, towards the end, he did.
B. Towards the end?
A. Well, at first he was fighting because you'd told him to. But then, towards the end, he began to enjoy it.

(a) I'm afraid he **lost**.
            didn't win
            was beaten
(b) The **point** is, did he put up a **good** fight, or didn't he?
    question   brave
(a) Oh, yes, he put up **a very** good fight.
            an extremely
               incredibly
                  extraordinarily
            quite a
            rather a

put up
(iv)

A. Don't tell me he's put the price up again!
B. No, this time he hasn't put the price up, he's cut down the number in a box.

(a) Don't tell me **he's** put (up) the **price** (up) again!
            the grocer's
              green-grocer
              coal merchant
              supplier
              wholesaler
(b) No, he's cut (down) the **number** in a **box** (down).
                  weight   packet
                            bag
                            carton
                            case
                            crate

put up
(v)*

A. I was thinking of putting it up for auction.
B. When were you thinking of putting it up?
A. Next month.
B. How much were you hoping to get for it?
A. How much were you thinking of offering for it?

(*a*) I was thinking of putting **it up** for   **auction**.
                       (up) my car (up) sale
                      house
                      transistor
(*b*) When **were** you **thinking of putting** it up?
        are   intending to put
                 hoping to put
(*a*) Next **month**.
      week
      Thursday

put up
(vi)

A. Now I have half of the capital I need, and all I have to do is to find someone to put up the other half.
B. Surely the Ministry will put up the other half?
A. No, this is what the Ministry says: they say that if I can find all the capital I need, and if my project proves a success, then they might help me to expand.

(*a*) All I have to do is to find someone **to put up**
                               who'll put up
                               willing to put up
                               able to put up
                               who's prepared to put up
    the other half.
            money
      the balance
      the rest of the capital
(*b*) Surely the **Ministry** will put (up) the **other half** (up)?
             Government   rest

155

put up
(vii)*

A. There are three serious candidates in the election – and then, of course, there's Herbert.
B. Oh, is Herbert putting himself up again?
A. He always puts himself up.
B. But he hasn't a hope of winning!
A. If he had, he wouldn't put up! I know Herbert!

(*a*) **Three** serious candidates have been put up.
   Two
(*b*) Is **Herbert** putting himself up again?
(*a*) He always puts himself up.

put up
(viii)*

A. We'd be glad to put him up for a week or or two – until he finds somewhere to live.
B. Are you quite sure, auntie? He keeps very late hours.
A. Well, we could certainly put him up for a day or two, no matter what hours he keeps.
B. And he has some very noisy friends, auntie.
A. Well, as I say, I've agreed to put him up for tonight, no matter how noisy his friends are.
B. And he doesn't like cats, auntie!

(*a*) We'd be glad to put **him** up for a **week** or two.
                         her   month
                                        day
(*b*) Are you quite sure, **auntie**?
                          uncle?
(*b*) **He keeps very late hours.**
   She has some very noisy friends
       doesn't like cats
       sleeps very late in the mornings
       takes all the bath water
       smokes a lot

156

put up
(ix)

A. If we miss the last train, we shall have to put up at Uncle Harry's for the night.
B. Should we need to telephone him first?
A. Oh, no – he always has plenty of room.
B. Do you put up there often?
A. Whenever I miss the last train.
B. He must be nice.
A. Who?
B. Your Uncle Harry.
A. He is nice. And so is his hotel. But it's a bit expensive. And he doesn't make any concessions to the family, unfortunately.

(a) We shall have to put up at Uncle **Harry's**.
(b) Do you often put up **there**?
              at your uncle's
              at his place
                  house
              at that hotel
(a) Whenever **I miss the last train**.
          it's too late to get home

rattle off

A. Gaunt is very impressive, isn't he?
B. He certainly has an impressive memory.
A. Yes – mention the Stock Market, and he can rattle off all the latest prices.
B. Or mention the railways and he can rattle off the time-table.
A. Or mention work – and he can rattle off a hundred good reasons why he shouldn't be doing any.

(b) Gaunt certainly has an **impressive** memory.
              incredible
              marvellous
              prodigious
(a) Yes – mention **the railways** and he can rattle (off) **the time-table** (off).
            Stock Market   latest prices
            football   latest scores
            cricket
            an old building   its history
            guest list   the names
            horse   its pedigree

read on　A. Excuse me, Miss Whistler, but I can't
　　　　　　　understand what this sentence means. That is,
　　　　　　　I can understand the words, but I don't see its
　　　　　　　connection with the rest of the story.
　　　　　　B. Well, Janet, its connection will become quite
　　　　　　　clear if you read on for a few more pages –
　　　　　　　if you read on to page seventeen, to be exact.

(a) Excuse me, **Miss Whistler**, but I can't understand this **sentence**.
　　　　Mr Brewster　　　　　　　　　　　　　phrase
　　　　　　　　　　　　　　　　　　　　　　word
　　　　　　　　　　　　　　　　　　　　　　speech
　　　　　　　　　　　　　　　　　　　　　　line
(b) If you read on **for a few more pages, Janet**, it'll become **quite** clear.
　　　　　　　to page seventeen　　　　　　　　　　absolutely
　　　　　　to the next chapter
　　　　　　　　end of the page
　　　　　　　　　　chapter

read up*　A. Who am I interviewing today, Paddy?
　　　　　　B. Professor Birkenshaw, June. He's an expert
　　　　　　　on fossils.
　　　　　　A. But I don't know anything about fossils!
　　　　　　B. Well, you have a whole morning in which to
　　　　　　　read up the subject and become an expert.
　　　　　　A. And where, if I may ask, shall I read it up?
　　　　　　B. At the Public Library, June – from a book.
　　　　　　A. Which book, Paddy?
　　　　　　B. A book on fossils, June.

(a) I don't know anything about **fossils**.
　　　　　　　　　flowers
　　　　　　　　　geology
　　　　　　　　　botany
(b) You have **a whole morning** to read (up) the subject (up)
　　　　　two hours
　　　　　a week

reckon up A. I suppose we'd better reckon up the total cost, and see if we caa afford to buy it.

B. I'm afraid if we do reckon it up, it'll seem far too expensive.

A. But we do want it, don't we? And we do need it?

B. Oh, let's order it, and not reckon up till it's too late to have second thoughts.

(a) I suppose we'd better reckon (up) **the total cost** (up).
> all the items
> the extra items
>> price of the extras
>> overheads
>> running costs
>> charges
>> fees

(b) I'm afraid if we do reckon it up, it'll seem **far too expensive**.
>   them   a lot   dear

reckon in A. But surely, when you costed the project, you reckoned in the hiring fee for this machinery, didn't you?

B. Well, you may remember that when I mentioned a hiring fee, I was told our own machinery would suffice. So I'm afraid that amount wasn't reckoned in at the time, no.

A. But it's obvious that our own machinery isn't enough! Who on earth told you such a stupid thing?

B. Hm! Er ... I hardly like to say!

(a) But surely you reckoned in the **hiring fee(s)**, didn't you?
>   cost of compensation
>   legal charges

(b) **That amount wasn't** reckoned in, no.
> Those items weren't
>> charges
>> fees

(a) Who told you such a stupid thing?

(b) I hardly like to say!

reel off**   A. So what did Gaunt do then?
               B. He reeled off the names of everyone who's
                   worked here for the last ten years.
               A. I hope he didn't reel off his own among
                   them!

(*a*) So what did **Gaunt** do **then**?

Hirst	after that
Insole	next
Judd	
Kemp	
Loney	
Moss	
Noble	
Ogden	
Potts	
Quinn	
Roe	
Small	
Tonks	
Vance	
Weeks	
Exley	
Young	
he	

(*b*) He reeled (off) all the **names** (off).

               figures
               results
               scores
               titles
               pedigrees

rig up   A. If you were ever stranded, do you think you
               could rig up a shelter?
               B. I'm hopeless with my hands, but I think I
                   could rig up a shelter of some kind, yes. But
                   it would probably collapse on top of me!

(*a*) Do you think you could rig up a **shelter**?

               hut
               boat

(*b*) I'm **hopeless** with my hands, but I think I could rig up a shelter
     not much good
            use

     of some kind, yes.
     of some sort

160

rub in*   A. When you were a boy, you said you could
              beat him at tennis. But you always lost.
            B. There's no need to rub it in.
            A. And you said you'd get the job. But, of
              course, he got it.
            B. I tell you, there's no need to rub it in!
            A. And actually, though I've no wish to rub it
              in, I told you he'd get the job.
            B. I remember that when we both proposed to
              you, it was me you chose.
            A. There's no need to rub that in.

(*a*) **You always lost**.
    He always beat you
    He got the job
    You didn't get the job
    You came second
    You're a failure
(*b*) **There's no need to rub it in**!
    You've no need to rub it in
    Stop rubbing it in
    No need to rub it in

rule out*   A. Would you rule out the use of force if all
                else fails?
              B. We hope reason will prevail.
              A. But if reason doesn't prevail, would you use
                force?
              B. We wouldn't rule out the possibility that
                force might be used if all else were to fail.

(*a*) Would you rule out the use of **force**?
                        fire-arms
                        weapons
                        artillery
                        bombs
(*b*) We hope **reason will prevail**.
            to reach a settlement
                an agreement
                terms satisfactory to both sides
                an amicable arrangement
            to find a peaceful solution

**run
down (i)***

A. The battery's run down. Would you mind giving me a push?
B. That battery seems to be permanently run down. It's time you got a new one.
A. Stop chattering and push, can't you?
B. I am pushing!
A. Harder! Can't you push harder? It's downhill – you should be able to push it easily enough.
B. Oh!
A. Push!
B. I can't push any harder!
A. Oops! Sorry about that! I forgot to release the handbrake. You haven't hurt yourself, have you?
B. Ooh!
A. Good. Push a bit more, then.

(a) The **battery**'s run down.
   power unit
(b) It seems to be **permanently run down**. It's time you **got a new one**.
   run down all the time   bought another one

**run
down
(ii)****

A. I'm not running her down, of course. But she's a dreadful gossip.
B. Oh, she gossips, does she? That's not nice, is it?
A. She does gossip. How the woman gossips! Never stops gossiping! Gossips all the time! Not that I want to run her down, of course. But she doesn't keep the house clean.
B. Oh, that's not very nice, is it?
A. And she doesn't look after the children properly – not in my opinion, she doesn't.
B. Well, I've no wish to run her down, either. But I must just tell you what Mrs Fisher said about her this morning.

(a) **I've no wish** to run her down, **of course**, but she's a **dreadful gossip**.
   I don't wish   you understand   scandal-monger
(b) Well, I've no wish to run her down either. But I must just tell you what **Mrs Fisher** said about her.

**run
down (iii)**

A. Carter's looking a bit run down after his illness. Tell him he mustn't be in too big a hurry to come back to work. Tell him to have another fortnight at least.
B. He does look terribly run down, yes. But he says he wants to start again next Monday.
A. Well, tell him he can't. You and I will be away on holiday, so there's nothing he can do.
B. Us? On holiday? Shall we?
A. Well, why not? You're looking a bit run down yourself. And I can't work here on my own, can I?

(a) **Carter**'s looking **a bit** run down after his **illness**.
   Miss Lowe   rather   her ordeal
               somewhat   operation
(b) **He** does look **terribly** run down, **yes**.
   She   awfully   you're right
               very   it's true
                           true enough

**run down
(iv)****

A. So at last we've run you down, Smith. We've found your hideout.
B. If I may say so, sir, you're very good at running escaped prisoners down, sir. No one runs down an escaped prisoner as well as you do, sir – no, sir, no one, sir – if I may say so, sir.
A. Oh, you made it easy for us, Smith. At least, during the last few days you did. Anyone would think you wanted to be recaptured, Smith.
B. Me, sir? How could you say such a thing, sir?
A. Even so, you ...
B. By the way, sir, what's for Christmas dinner this year? Same as usual, sir?

(a) So **at last we've** run you down, **Smith**.
      we've finally
(b) You're very good at running (down) **escaped prisoners** (down), sir.
                                      convicts
                     criminals

163

run down
(v)*

A. William, I don't want to be a back-seat driver – but you nearly ran that lady down.
B. Nonsense, my dear, she saw me coming. I've never run anyone down in my life, as you very well know.
A. But they do say, dear, there's always a first time for everything.
B. Look out, you fool! Look where you're going! Why doesn't the fool look where he's going!
A. It is a pedestrian crossing, dear!

(*a*) You nearly ran that **lady** down.
(*b*) I've never run anyone down in my life, as **you very well know.**
                           you know very well
                           you should know
(*a*) There's always a first time for everything.

run in
(i)

A. Daddy, it says 'Running in, please pass' in the back window of that car. What does 'running in' mean, daddy?
B. It means the car has a new engine that needs to be driven slowly for a few hundred miles.
A. But he's just passed us, daddy, and we're doing sixty!
B. Perhaps he's run it in already, and forgotten to remove the sticker from the window.
A. Yes.
B. Or perhaps it isn't his car!

(*a*) He's just **passed** us, and we're doing **sixty.**
         overtaken   fifty
(*b*) Perhaps **he's run it in already.**
               already run it in
               not bothering to run it in properly
         it's not his car
         he's forgotten to remove the sticker
         he hasn't remembered to remove the sticker

run in

(ii)*

A. Look out, you fool!
B. Look out, you fool!
A. Why don't you look where you're going?
B. Why don't you look where you're going?
A. You deserve to be run down!
B. You ought to be run in!
A. Run down, that's what you deserve to be!
B. Run in, that's what you ought to be!
A. Ah, Officer, I'm glad you've come.
B. I'm very glad you've come, Officer.
A. You see, I was driving along carefully, when suddenly this fool . . .
B. I was crossing carefully, when suddenly this fool came out . . .

(a) You deserve to be **run down**!
 over
 knocked down
(b) You **ought to** be run in!
 should
(a) Run down, that's what you deserve to be!

run out

(i)**

A. To tell you the truth, Officer, I didn't know it'd run out.
B. Well, as you can see, sir, this licence ran out a month ago.
A. Yes, you're quite right, of course. I'll er . . . I'll renew it straight away . . . er, at the post office.
B. You do that, sir. And if you wouldn't mind taking it to the police station at two o'clock this afternoon, sir, I should like to have a look at it.
A. But Officer, two o'clock isn't convenient for me, I'm afraid.
B. And no other time is convenient for me, sir, I'm afraid. So shall we say two o'clock, sir?

(a) I **didn't know** it'd run out, Officer.
 realize my licence
 wasn't aware car licence
(b) It ran out **a month** ago, sir, as you can see.
 two weeks madam

165

run out

(ii)

A. Susan, it's a lovely party. Can I do anything to help?

B. The lemonade's almost run out. Could you fetch some more? Wait a minute, I'll give you some money.

A. Oh, no, let me get this. What about the beer, by the way? We don't want that to run out!

B. Oh, there's no need to worry about the beer. John bought enough for an army. There's no danger of the beer running out when John's around!

(a) Can I do anything to help?

(b) The **lemonade**'s almost run out.
     fruit juice
     orange squash
     lime cordial

(a) What about the **beer**?
        wine
        whisky

(b) There's no danger of the **beer** running out!
           cider

run out

(iii)*

A. My patience is just about running out!

B. Now sit down and have a nice cup of tea, and tell me all about it.

A. I try to be patient with Nicholas. I try to help him. I try to encourage him. I try to ...

B. He says he's tried to be patient with you.

A. With me?

B. But his patience is running out, he says.

A. He dares to say that about his father! Just wait till ...

B. And I'm rapidly losing my patience with both of you!

(a) My patience **is just about running out**!
           has just about run out
           is just about exhausted

(b) **Nicholas** says **his** is running out **too**. And I'm losing my patience with
   Veronica   hers   as well
both of you!

166

run out

(iv)

A. This is the point where the pipes run out into the sea. Here, can you see it on the map?

B. Ah, yes, I see.

A. And as long as they run out here, rather than there, we can't hope to have satisfactory beaches here, can we?

(*a*) This is the point where the pipes run out into the sea.
　　　　　　place　at which drains　　　　　　river
　　　　　　　　　　　　　 waste
　　　　　　　　　　　　　 sewage　　　runs
　　　　　　　　　　　　　 effluence

(*b*) Ah, yes, I see.

run out

(v)

A. When the pressure's high, Mr Burton, the water leaks through here and runs out all over the place.

B. I'll do a temporary repair now, Mrs Thorne, and I'll come back next week and do it properly.

A. But if the pressure increases in the meantime, will the water run out?

B. It shouldn't run out, I don't think, no.

(*a*) The water runs out all over the place.
　　　 oil　　　　　　　　 floor
　　　 paraffin　　　　　 kitchen
　　　 petrol　　　　　　 room
　　　 liquid　　　　　　 house

(*b*) I'll do a temporary repair, then it shouldn't run out.
　　　　　　　　　　　　　　 won't
　　　　　　　　　　　　　　 oughtn't to

see off

(i)*

A. It was good of them to come and see us off, wasn't it?

B. On the whole I prefer people not to come to the station. But, even so, as you say, it was extremely good of them to see us off.

A. I'm glad we have the carriage all to ourselves.

B. So am I.

A. I want to have a good cry.

B. Yes, a good cry would do us both good. And it's nothing to be ashamed of.

(*a*) It was good of **them** to see us off, wasn't it?
> John and Sue
> father and mother
> our friends
> > colleagues
>
> him
> her
> Jim
> Meg

I want to have a good cry!
I need to have
I need
I'm going to have a good weep
I must blow my nose
> dry my eyes

see off

(ii)

A. I've already told him to keep off my land. See him off, Jake! See him off!

B. Shall I take the dog?

A. Take the bull, if you like, Jake, as long as you see him right off my land.

(*a*) See **him** off, **Jake**! See him off!
> the man
> chap
> fellow

(*b*) Shall I **take the dog**?
> Bruce
> Wolf
> Barker
> set the dogs on him?

(*a*) **Take the bull if you like.**
> Set the bull on him, if you like

168

see off
(iii)*

A. I'm sure you won't allow me to say Nicholas is greedy, but . . .
B. He does like his food, I'll admit.
A. But he's seen off all the chicken!
B. Well, I . . .
A. And he's seen off most of the cheese!
B. Ah! Well, I've bought you a special pie, dear. And, if you like, you can see it off all by yourself. That is, unless you can spare a small piece for me.

(*a*) He's seen (off) **all the chicken** (off).
       meat
       fish
     most of the cheese
(*b*) Well, I've **bought you** a special **pie**, dear. You can see it off all by
    made you   cake
          dish
          meal

  yourself.

see
through

A. I've started the job, Mabel, and I'm going to see it through to the end.
B. You're not in a fit state to see anything through, Peter. You're not well enough to go. Alec'll supervise the job for you, surely.
A. Over my dead body!
B. But what's wrong with Alec? I'm sure he's a . . .
A. Nothing – as long as he's minding his own business. But this is my business.

(*a*) **I'm going** to see the **job** through to the **end**.
  I intend   work   finish
        task
        project
        plan
        scheme
(*b*) You're **not well** enough to see it through, **Peter**.
   aren't fit

169

set off
(i)*

A. As you see, this delicate bracelet will set off your elegant hand beautifully!
B. Perhaps it would – but I'm afraid it's not my hand it's intended for, it's my aunt's.
A. Oh!
B. And her hands are her worst feature.
A. Then perhaps this superb necklace!
B. Yes, it is rather fine. Yes – and it'd set off her neck very well. Mm. It would. She has a lovely neck.
A. Then perhaps . . .
B. But of course, I couldn't possibly afford it.

(*a*) This **bracelet** will set (off) your **hand** (off) **beautifully**.

	wrist	superbly
necklace	neck	
	shoulders	
ring	hand	

(*b*) But I'm afraid it's not my **hand** it's intended for, it's **my aunt's**.

friend's
Madeleine's

set off
(ii)

A. Everything was going very well – we were all keeping straight faces – when John set us all off giggling.
B. Oh dear me! Mr Wadsworth wouldn't like that!
A. Well, John set me off, and I set June off, and before we knew where we were. . . . We just couldn't stop!
B. So that was what set him off!
A. Doing what?
B. I heard him talking to the Headmaster – who, by the way, seems to be striding rather purposefully in this direction.

(*a*) John set us all off **giggling**.
laughing
sniggering
fooling about

(*b*) Oh dear me! Mr **Wadsworth** wouldn't like that!
Wordsworth
Wentworth
Wigglesworth

set off
(iii)*

A. We'll set off in an hour.
B. We'll set off now.
A. We'll set off in half an hour.
B. We'll set off now.
A. We'll set off soon – very soon.
B. Now – just now.
A. Now?
B. Now.

(a) We'll set off **in an hour**.
           half an hour
           a short time
           a while
        soon
        shortly
        very shortly
(b) We'll set off now.
(a) Now?
(b) Now.

set off
(iv)

A. When are you going to set off your fireworks?
B. After you've set yours off.
A. No – you have to set yours off first.
B. Let's be reasonable.
A. Yes, we must be reasonable.
B. Let's compromise.
A. It's always necessary to compromise.
B. Set one of yours off first, then I'll set off one of mine.
A. Set one of yours off first.

(a) When are you going to set (off) your **fireworks** (off)?
                                    crackers
                                    rockets
                                    bangers
(b) **After** you've set yours off. Let's **be reasonable**.
     When   compromise
     As soon as   come to an agreement
                                            understanding
                                            a satisfactory arrangement
(a) Yes, we must **be reasonable**.
                 compromise

171

set off
(v)*

A. I'm afraid your article's set off a very fierce controversy.
B. That's why I wrote it.
A. It's set off a chain of events that might prove embarrassing.
B. That's why I wrote it.
A. It's set off a lot of complaints both from the public, and here in the office.
B. As I say, that's why I wrote it.
A. So what I have to say to you, I take it, will come as no surprise.

(a) I'm afraid your **article**'s set off a **fierce controversy**.

book	argument
play	lot of complaints
	adverse comment
	criticism

(b) **That's why I wrote it**.
That was my intention
That was my reason for writing it
That's what I had in mind when I wrote it
That was the idea
That's the idea

show off
(i)

A. Christopher's very clever, I agree. But he's always showing off. Why must he always show off so much?
B. He has plenty to show off about, of course.
A. Yes. Yes, but when you're as clever as that, and everyone knows how clever you are, then, surely, there's no need to show off, is there?

(a) Why must **he** always show off **so much**?

she	to that extent
	as much as that
	like that
	all the time

(b) **He** has **plenty** to show off about, of course.
She   a great deal

(a) Yes. Yes, but when everyone knows how **clever** you are,

         bright
         brilliant

there's no need to show off, is there?
       necessity
it isn't necessary to show off, is it

172

show off

(ii)

A. I know you want to go to the regatta, and I know you want to take me in your new car. But I'd like to know one other thing.

B. What's that?

A. Which of us are you wanting to show off – me or the car?

B. You, of course.

A. Be honest, John!

B. All right – both of you. And don't ask me to be more honest than that, Jane!

(a) I'd like to know one **other** thing.
          more
(b) What's that?
(a) Which of us are you wanting to show off – me or **the car**?
                                        boat
                                        yacht
                                        your new suit

show up

(i)*

A. Sir Harvey hasn't shown up yet.

B. He never does show up on time for a performance. It's seven o'clock already, and every seat is full.

A. The fellow's a nuisance, an absolute nuisance. Why can't he be punctual? Why can't he show up on time?

B. He's not only a nuisance, he's a . . . Ah, good evening, Sir Harvey!

A. Sir Harvey! So glad you were able to get here, Sir Harvey! Oh, no, no, no, There's plenty of time, plenty of time, Sir Harvey. I was just telling my colleague here that . . .

(a) Sir **Harvey** hasn't shown up **yet**.
      Ben   so far
(b) He never shows up **on time for a performance**.
                      at the theatre in time
                      at the proper time
                      until the last minute
                      till the very last moment
(a) The **fellow's** a **nuisance**, an absolute **nuisance**.
      chap   menace   liability

show up
(ii)*

A. I know the waiter made a mistake about the bill. But there was no need to show me up in the restaurant the way you did! Waving the bill about, and shouting like that!

B. I didn't show you up! It was him I showed up!

A. You showed me up, and you showed yourself up, as well!

B. Driver! Driver! You've gone past the end of our road! I said Clifton Road – that was Clifton Road. Don't expect me to pay the extra fare! No, no – you'll have to turn round. I thought you taxi-drivers were supposed to know your way about! No, not Shipton Road, Clifton Road! CLIFTON ROAD!

(*a*) There was no need to show me up **in the restaurant** the way you did!
                             at the party
                                  reception
(*b*) I didn't show you up!
(*a*) You showed me up, and you showed yourself up as well!

show up
(iii)*

A. I think the pink marble shows up very well against the dark blue background.

B. I think it would show up rather better against a green background.

A. But we haven't got a green wall, and we have got a dark blue one. And I think it shows up extremely well there.

B. But you've never seen it against a green one. You've no imagination, that's your trouble.

A. Neither have you.

B. No imagination?

A. No – you've never seen it against a green background either.

(*a*) I think the **pink** **marble** shows up **very** well there.
              white stone   rather
              black metal   extremely
              gold centrepiece   particularly
(*b*) You've no **imagination**!
              taste

shut up

(i)

A. Tony, I'd like to go and watch the match. Shut up the shop for me, will you? Shut up now, if you like – you know where to leave the key.

B. Yes. Enjoy yourself.

A. Bye!

B. Bye! I think I will shut up now. I wouldn't mind going to the match myself, actually. Now, where are we? Er ... here – it should be here. Hello, it isn't here either. Nor here. And it isn't here! Hey, Tony! Tony, I know where to leave it. But where is it? Tony! Tony! Hey, Tony, where's the key? How can I shut the shop up without a key? Tony!

(a) Shut (up) the **shop** (up) for me, **will you?**
           store   won't you?
           place   there's a good chap!

(b) **Yes.**   **Enjoy yourself.**
   Of course I will Have a good time

(a) Bye!

(b) Bye!

shut up

(ii)

A. Shut up for a moment, Liz, I'm trying to listen! I thought I could hear ...

B. But mummy, I want to ...

A. I told you to shut up! How can I listen, if you talk? Shut her up, daddy, can't you?

B. But mummy, I think I'm ...

A. I thought I told you to shut up! Shut up, please! Now – is he ... No. No, he isn't. I thought I could hear the baby crying, but he isn't. No, he's not crying. It's all right. He's quiet. Now, Liz, what was it you wanted to say? Oh, Liz, no! No, don't be sick all over the carpet! Daddy, why couldn't you ... Oh, Liz, really! Liz, why didn't you tell me?

(a) Shut up for a **moment, Liz.** Shut her up, **daddy,** can't you?
          minute   John
          second

(b) But mummy!

slip up

A. You've slipped up, haven't you?
B. Slipped up?
A. You've slipped up.
B. How've I slipped up?
A. You said you hadn't used the car, didn't you?
B. Well?
A. Whose is this cigarette lighter, then?
B. Where did you find it?
A. I'll give you one guess.

(a) You've slipped up, haven't you?
(b) How've I slipped up?
(a) Whose is this **cigarette lighter**?
           glove
           wallet
           handbag
           handkerchief
           briefcase
           car key
(b) Where did you find it?
(a) I'll give you one guess.

speak up (i)

A. Would you mind speaking up, please. We can't hear what you're saying, at the back.
B. I'm sorry, what did you say?
A. Speak up, can't you?
B. Sorry. But I still can't quite catch what you say.
A. I'm asking you to . . .
B. Would you mind speaking up, please?

(a) Would you mind speaking up, please?
(b) I'm sorry, **what did you say**?
           do you say
           are you saying
        what's that you're saying
        what's that you say
        what was that
(a) **Speak up, can't you**?
  I was asking you to speak up
  Can't you speak up

**speak up/
out (ii)**

A. Daddy, they're all wanting to do something naughty. But they mustn't, it's wrong! I know it's wrong!

B. Then you must tell them, Margaret.

A. Yes, daddy, but if I tell them, they won't like me any more.

B. Sometimes we have to speak out and say what's right, dear, no matter what anyone thinks.

A. But if I do speak up about it, they might . . .

B. Well, keep quiet if you like. But one day you might wish you'd spoken out.

(*a*) But if I speak out **about it,**   **they won't like me.**
                    against them   they'll hate me
                                    think I'm a sneak

(*b*) Sometimes we have to speak up for **our beliefs.**
                                    what we believe
                                    what we think is right

spin out*

A. And in a few moments, ladies and gentlemen, we shall see the film, and I hope you . . .

B. Hey! Mr Slingsby, spin out your introduction a bit, will you? The film's snapped. It needs splicing. Tell them about your most embarrassing moment, or about . . . oh, tell them anything, as long as you spin it out!

A. Well, er, as I was saying, ladies and gentlemen, we shall be seeing the film before very long – er . . . quite soon, in fact, we shall be seeing it. But, er, first of all, I thought, er, you might perhaps like to hear a little story. Er, one day, it was a Thursday, I remember. Yes, er, it was a Thursday, er, in September. I remember it was in September because, I clearly recall that on that . . .

(*b*) Spin (out) your introduction (out) **a bit.**
                                    for a moment or two

(*a*) Well, as I was saying, ladies and gentlemen, we shall be seeing the

film	**before very long.**
picture	shortly
slides	quite soon

177

split up

(i)

A. I think I'd like to split you up into groups now. Do you do group work often?

B. Yes, sir.

A. And how does Mrs Berry split you up, usually?

B. Usually we split up into four groups.

A. Shall I split you up into three for a change?

B. No, thank you, sir. We like four best.

(a) I'd like to split you up into groups now. How does **Mrs Berry** usually split you up?

(b) Usually, we split up into **four** groups.

(a) Shall I split you up into **three** for a change?

(b) No thank you. We like **four** best.

split up

(ii)

A. Whatever happened to Back and Forth?

B. Billy Back and Frankie Forth! What a pair of comedians! What a comical pair they were!

A. Whatever happened to them?

B. Oh, they split up, you know.

A. No, I didn't know.

B. Yes, they split up, oh, five or six years ago. Yes, I remember Forth went into some kind of business – very successful – and Back ... Back stayed on the stage. But he didn't make much progress as a solo turn. And I don't know what happened to him after that.

A. But they don't breed comedians like them any more, do they? Back and Forth! How they made me laugh! What a pity it was they split up. Billy Back and Frankie Forth! What a shame!

(b) **Back and Forth** split up, you know.
    To and Fro
    There and Back
    In and Out
    Up and Down

(a) No, I didn't know.

(b) Yes, they split up, oh, **five or six** years ago.

(a) **What a shame!**
       pity
   How sad

**stick
out (i)**

A. It's rude to stick out your tongue!
B. I wasn't sticking it out at you, daddy.
A. You were sticking it out, and that's rude.
B. But not at you, daddy.
A. Who were you sticking it out at?
B. Not at anyone. Daddy, can you touch your nose with your tongue?

(a) It's **very** rude to stick (out) your tongue (out).
 awfully
 dreadfully
 terribly
(b) I wasn't sticking it out at you, **daddy**.
 mummy
 dad
 mum
 grannie

**stick
out (ii)***

A. He's presented this land to the school, and he's given a fortune to charity.
B. But his motive sticks out a mile!
A. His motive?
B. It sticks out a mile that he's hoping to be elected next year. Will you give him your vote?
A. But it shows he's generous, surely?
B. Will you vote for him?
A. Oh, no. No, I never actually thought of voting for him, I don't think.

(b) His **motive** sticks out a mile!
 reason for doing it
 real aim
 true intention
(a) His motive?
(b) It sticks out a mile.

stick (it) out (iii)

A. It took a lot of patience and stamina, and a lot of hard work. But he stuck the course out to the end, and now, I'm glad to say, he's done very well in the examination.

B. You must be very proud of him.

A. I've always been proud of young Nick, you know. And the way he's stuck this out has confirmed the belief I've always had in him. Yes, I've always thought I was a lucky man to have a son like Nicholas.

(a) He stuck **it** out to the **end**.
           the course finish
           training last
           classes
           tests
(b) You must be very **proud of him**.
           pleased with him
           happy about him
           happy for him
(a) I've always thought I was **lucky** to have a **son** like **Nick**.
           fortunate   boy   Chris
                             Dick
                             Ted

stir up*

A. There's bound to be trouble.

B. And if there is, I suppose you'll stir it up even more.

A. Stir it up? Surely you know me better than that! Would I stir up trouble?

B. Let's put it this way: you wouldn't willingly allow it to subside, would you?

(a) There's bound to be **trouble**.
           strong feeling
           a lot of emotion
           ill-feeling
(b) And if there is,   **I suppose** you'll stir it up even more.
           should be   imagine
(a) Surely you know me better than that!

sum up

(i)

A. Well, ladies and gentlemen, you've heard both sides of the argument. All that remains for me to do is to try to sum up what the speakers have just said.
B. Lunch!
A. What d'you say?
B. After lunch!
A. Ah, yes. And after I've summed up, we can, of course, all go to lunch.

(*a*) All that remains for me to do is to try to sum up

what the speakers have said.
what's been said
the arguments
the points made
the two points of view
the views expressed
the two sides of the argument

(*b*) After **lunch!**
dinner

sum up

(ii)

A. I summed the fellow up straight away, of course.
B. Oh, she did sum him up! Katie's very good at summing people up, you know, John.
A. I knew he was a crook. I knew the moment I saw him.
B. She knew, John. She summed him up immediately, you know!
A. I knew he was a confidence trickster.
B. Oh, she knew he didn't really own a gold mine, you know.
A. He was a rogue, an absolute rogue!
B. She knew she'd never see her money again, John.
A. An absolute villain!
B. And she hasn't – of course!

(*a*) I summed the fellow up **straight away.**
          villain   immediately
          situation

(*b*) **Katie's** very **good** at summing **people up.**
          clever   up the situation
          quick

181

summon up (i)

A. He's the strongest man in the world, I should think.
B. Well, he'll need to summon up all his strength and all his courage if he's going to lift my elephant.
A. She's quite a large elephant, actually.
B. Look how he's straining! See his muscles bulging as he summons up all his strength! But he'll have to try to summon up more – he's not making much of an impression on her.
A. Oh, now see what's happened!
B. Put him down, Princess! Princess, put him down!

(b) He'll need to summon (up) all his **courage** (up).
                strength
                will-power
                energy
                skill
                expertise
(a) She's quite a large elephant, **actually**.
                in fact
                as a matter of fact

summon up (ii)*

A. This is a difficult decision for me to make. Too difficult for me to make alone. I shall have to summon up the spirit of my great-great-grandfather.
B. Can you summon up spirits, then?
A. Only the spirit of my great-great-grandfather.
B. Was he very wise?
A. Oh, no, he wasn't particularly wise, I don't think. But, as I said, his is the only spirit I know how to summon up. Now, quiet, please. I must have absolute silence, if you don't mind. Sh!

(a) I must summon (up) the **spirit** of my **grandfather** (up).
                      ghost   ancestor
(b) Can you summon (up) **spirits** (up) then?
                      ghosts
(a) Only the **spirit** of my **grandfather**.
                ghost

182

**take
aback****

A. I was quite taken aback when I saw him.
B. Why should you have been taken aback?
There's nothing at all surprising about
Brown.
A. But I thought he was dead!
B. I don't know how you got that idea! Brown
never was very much alive, of course. But, no,
he's certainly not dead.

(*a*) I was **quite** taken aback.
       greatly
       very much
       completely
       somewhat
(*b*) Why should you have been taken aback?

**take in
(i)***

A. Have you a room to spare?
B. A room to spare? I don't know what you're
talking about!
A. Oh, but I thought you had rooms to let. I
was told you take in lodgers.
B. Take in lodgers? Lodgers, in my house?
A. I'm terribly sorry – I must've been
misinformed. I'll, er, I'll try somewhere else.
Sorry.
B. Wait, young man! Just wait a moment,
please – as I said, I don't under any
circumstances take in lodgers. But I do
occasionally – only occasionally, mind – er,
take in guests. Paying guests, that is. And
it just so happens that at the moment I
happen to have a room vacant. And if a
suitable guest – such as yourself, for
instance – were to present himself, then I
might consider, er . . . Would you like to see
the room?

(*a*) I was told you take in **lodgers**.
                boarders
(*b*) Take lodgers in! In my house? I do **occasionally** take in paying guests.
                               sometimes
                               from time to time

take in
(ii)

A. Katie was completely taken in by him, weren't you, dear?
B. I knew he was a rogue, of course.
A. He took her in completely, John. Poor Katie! He told her he owned a gold mine, you know, John.
B. A crook! He was an absolute villain!
A. And he sold her some shares in this gold mine.
B. All right, so he sold me the shares – but what about the time when you were ...
A. I admit it. I admit it – I've been taken in in my time, too.
B. Well, then, why are you ...
A. But not as completely as that. Isn't Katie marvellous, John?

(*a*) Katie was **completely** taken in by **him**.
　　　　　　utterly　　　　　　　　the man
　　　　　　　　　　　　　　　　　　fellow
(*b*) But what about **the time** when you were taken in?
　　　　　　　　　　　occasion
　　　　　　　　　　that time

take in
(iii)

A. Have you managed to take in what I've said so far? It's rather a difficult process to explain, I'm afraid.
B. Well, I haven't taken in all the detail, of course. But I think I've got the gist of it, thank you.
A. All right, then – we'll go on to the next stage.

(*a*) Have you managed to take in **what I've said**?
　　　　　　　　　　　　　　　　　my explanation
　　　　　　　　　　　　　　　　　　theory
　　　　　　　　　　　　　　　　all the facts
　　　　　　　　　　　　　　　this difficult idea
(*b*) I haven't taken (in) all the detail (in), of course. But I think I've got

　　the gist of it.
　　the general idea

take in
(iv)

A. Would this new boundary line take in both
   of these villages, or only one?
B. It'd take them both in.
A. I see.
B. Don't you think the larger unit will be much
   more convenient, though, administratively
   speaking?
A. Administratively speaking, yes. But humanly
   speaking, I'm not quite so sure.

(*a*) Would this **boundary line** take in **both of these villages**?
    new scheme   this town
    arrangement   lake
                      private housing
                      housing estate
                      agricultural land
                      area

(*b*) **Yes, it would**.
    It would, yes
    Yes
    It would

take in
(v)

A. Those trousers, sergeant.
B. Sir?
A. And that jacket, sergeant.
B. Sir?
A. They need taking in.
B. Yes, sir!
A. They're distinctly baggy, sergeant. Have
   them taken in.
B. Yes, sir!
A. Are they new, sergeant, or have you been on
   a diet?
B. Yes, sir!

(*a*) **Those trousers need** taking in.
    That jacket   needs
          waist
          waist-band
          skirt
(*b*) Yes, **sir**!
    Mr Smith
    Miss Lacey
(*a*) Have **them** taken in.
         it

take in
(vi)

A. I refuse to allow you to make rude remarks about either of them! I know as well as anyone else that they both have their limitations. But kindly keep your remarks to yourself!

B. But I was only pointing out that they don't always pay their rent promptly.

A. Mr and Mrs Davy took me in when my father died and when my mother was in hospital. I had no relatives, no one in the world! And Mr and Mrs Davy took me in out of the kindness of their hearts.

B. But I was merely trying . . .

A. So don't expect me to listen to any criticism of them!

(*a*) Mr and Mrs Davy took me in when **my father died**.
                                 I was left without parents
                                 I lost both my parents

(*b*) But I was **only** trying to **point out** that they don't
              merely   tell you

   pay their rent punctually.
      rates promptly
  keep the house very clean

take off
(i)

A. You'd better be careful about what you say to Chadwick.

B. Why should I be careful? He's only a little fellow.

A. He's a marvellous mimic, you know. And he can be quite devastating when he takes someone off. He might decide to do a take-off of you – and if he does, he'll make a laughing stock of you.

B. Well, yes – he might take me off once. But if he does, it'll be the last take-off he'll be in a position to do for a very long time!

(*a*) He might decide to **do a take-off of you**.
                      take you off
(*b*) If he takes me off, it'll be the last take-off he'll **be in a position to do**.
                                        able to do
                                        ever do

take off
(ii)

A. I thought it was one of the best radio series I've ever heard. Why on earth have they taken it off?

B. They haven't taken it off as far as I know. But I think they have changed the time of the programme. Isn't it on tomorrow?

A. Ah, let's see. Yes. Yes, you're right. It is on tomorrow. Well, if they had taken it off, I should've written a very strong letter indeed.

B. But as they haven't, perhaps you might enjoy a drop of this?

(*a*) Why have they taken the series off?
     that documentary
      news programme
      children's programme
      comedy show
(*b*) They haven't taken it off, as far as I know.

take off
(iii)

A. She's nearly ready, Mr Grant. But do take your coat off for a few minutes, won't you – it's so hot today, isn't it?

B. I won't take it off, Mrs Sharpe, if you don't mind.

A. Are you quite sure – you must be boiling in that overcoat!

B. Quite sure, thank you. I'm still feeling the cold after my trip abroad, you know.

A. Oh, have you been abroad, Mr Grant?

B. For seven months, Mrs Sharpe. Do you mean to say you hadn't noticed?

A. Oh, you mustn't mind me, Mr Grant. I have a memory like a sieve, and my daughter...

B. I quite understand, Mrs Sharpe.

(*b*) I won't take (off) my coat (off), if you don't mind.
      hat
      scarf
      gloves
(*a*) Are you quite sure?
(*b*) Quite sure, thank you.

take off (iv)

A. But I have paid cash, and I have paid promptly, and it is a very big amount, and I am a regular customer.

B. Yes, sir.

A. Well, aren't you going to take anything off the bill? Aren't you going to giv me a discount?

B. I'm afraid I'm not allowed to give any discount, sir. But perhaps you'd like to have a word with Mr Benson, sir – he might take off a pound or two.

A. And then again he might not! I know Mr Benson only too well, I'm afraid!

B. There's no harm in trying, though, sir, is there?

A. And there's no point in trying, either – not with Benson, there isn't.

(*a*) Aren't you going to take anything off the **bill**?

$$\text{total}$$
$$\text{price}$$
$$\text{retail price}$$

(*b*) **Mr Benson** might take (off) a **pound or two** (off).

$$\text{dollar}$$

(*a*) I know **Mr Benson** only too well, I'm **afraid**

$$\text{sorry to say}$$

take off (v)

A. The plane took off beautifully and exactly on time, but just after the take-off, the pilot noticed that one of the instruments wasn't working properly. So he had to land again.

B. Oh, I see! So this is the second time the plane's taken off. I thought it was most unusual for that particular plane to be late.

A. It's most unusual for any of our planes to be late.

(*a*) The **plane** took off **beautifully** and **exactly on time**.

aircraft ·   very smoothly punctually
helicopter   at the scheduled time

(*b*) Oh, I see! So this is the second time it's taken off.

188

take over

(i)

A. Does this arrangement suit everybody, then?
B. I think so, yes. Let me see if I've got it right:
   I take over from Ann at eleven, you take over
   from me at one o'clock, and John takes over
   from you at three.
A. That's it. But, as I said, I've an appointment
   at twelve, so I may not be able to take over
   from you at exactly one o'clock.
B. What about your lunch, by the way? Shall we
   ask them to keep it for you – or shall I get
   you a sandwich, or something?
A. It's a lunch appointment, actually.

(b) I take over from Ann at eleven.
    John takes   me   one o'clock
(a) That's it.
          right

take

over (ii)

A. It's a shame to see all these fine little
   businesses being taken over by the industrial
   giants, isn't it?
B. Oh, I don't know. It's realistic and efficient.
   I wouldn't mind if someone took us over – a
   take-over bid would be very good for our firm.
A. What company would you like to be taken
   over by? That's if you had the choice.
B. Which we haven't! Well, now, let me see . . .

(b) I wish someone would take (over) our firm (over).
                                  business
                                  company
                                  concern
                                  factory
(a) What company would you like to be taken over by? That's if you had
      corporation
   the choice.

(b) Which we haven't!

talk over A. I'll be quite honest with you, Nicholas. And
I'm pleased you've talked the problem over
with me. And I do think it's the sort of job
you'd do very well. But don't you think you
should talk the whole question over with your
father first?
B. I've talked it over with father, and he
approves.
A. He does?

(a) Don't you think you should talk the **matter** over with your **father**?
                                           question   mother
                                             subject   boss
                                             problem   parents
                                                                         relatives

(b) I've talked it over with **him**, and **he approves.**
                                        her   she
                                           them   they approve
                                                                think it's a good idea

**talk
round*** A. Nicholas tells me he talked it over with you
and that you approve.
B. Yes, I do approve. I didn't approve at first,
as a matter of fact. But in the end he
managed to talk me round.
A. Oh, he didn't say he'd had to talk you round.
B. He doesn't tell you everything, you know!

(b) **In the end** he managed to talk me round.
   At last
   Finally
(a) Oh, he didn't **say he'd had** to talk you round.
                    tell me it'd been necessary
(b) **He** doesn't tell you everything, you know!
   Nicholas
   Your son

tell off

A. I think it was rather a witty thing to have said, don't you?

B. I don't know about witty! I think it was extremely cheeky. If I were his father, I'd give him a good telling off! A good telling off – that's what he needs! And more than a telling off, he needs a good hiding! Was that all he said about me?

A. There was one other thing. Would you like to hear?

(a) I think it was a **witty** thing to have said.
      clever
      smart
      shrewd
      penetrating

(b) I think it was extremely **cheeky**. That boy **needs a good telling off!**
      impertinent   wants telling off
      impudent   ought to be told off
      rude   should be given a good telling off
      facetious

think over

A. I'm not going to decide now, Andrew. I'll have to think it over.

B. But you've been thinking it over for a month already! Surely you've had plenty of time to think it over! Can't you make a decision?

A. I can, yes. But I don't intend to. Not yet, anyway.

(a) I'll have to think the **matter** over.
      question
      subject
      problem
      idea

(b) Surely you've had **plenty of** time to think it over!
      lots of
      ample

191

think up   A. Now listen to me, Gregory! The boss is coming this afternoon. You'd better think up an explanation, you'd better think it up quickly, and it'd better be a good one.

B. I don't need to think up any sort of story – the facts speak for themselves.

A. The facts do speak for themselves. But not in the way you seem to imagine.

B. I don't need to . . .

A. Of course, it's your business! Please yourself! But don't say I didn't tell you!

(a) You'd better think up **an explanation**.
                       excuse
                    some sort of a story
                         tale

(b) **I've no need** to think up any sort of **story**. The facts speak for themselves.
    I don't   explanation
    There's no need for me   excuse
                             tale

throw out (i)   A. It's a sensible proposal.

B. It is sensible. But they'll throw it out.

A. Throw it out? Why?

B. Because nobody's ready for it. It's ahead of its time.

(b) They'll throw the **proposal** out.
                      idea
                      scheme
                      plan
                      proposition

(a) Throw it out? **Why**?
                      Why should they do that
                      Why should they throw it out
                      Why should they want to throw it out
                      Why do you say that?
                      Why do you think so?

(b) Because it's ahead of its time.

throw

out (ii)*

A. I threw out a few suggestions, and the Chairman threw out an idea or two, and, on the whole, the meeting went very well, I think.

B. You and the Chairman!

A. Well, the Chairman and I, shall we say.

(a) I threw out a few **suggestions**, and so did the **Chairman**.
     ideas   President
     proposals   Principal
             Prime Minister

(b) You and the Chairman!

(a) Well, the Chairman and I, **shall we say**.
       if you like
       if you'd prefer it that way
       to put it another way

throw

out (iii)

A. Really! This machinery's hopeless! It's antiquated, it's clumsy, it's inefficient, it's dirty, and it's . . .

B. And it's time we threw it out.

A. It is time we threw it out, yes. Oh, Mr Barton, I didn't know it was you. I didn't hear you coming. I was talking to myself about the . . .

B. I heard you. And I agree. It is time we threw it out – as I said – if you heard me.

(b) It's time we threw **this machinery** out.
       these machines
       this equipment
        tackle
       these tools

(a) It is time we threw it out, **yes**.
        I agree
        you're right
        it's true

throw out (iv)

A. It's a very small lamp, yes. But it throws out out a very powerful beam. See.

B. Oh, yes. Yes. That's quite good enough for the purpose, isn't it?

A. More than good enough, I should've thought.

B. Who'd've believed a little thing like that could throw out such a light!

(*a*) It throws out a very **powerful beam**.
                 big light
                 strong heat
(*b*) Oh, yes. Yes. That's **quite** good enough for the purpose.
                perfectly
                entirely
(*a*) More than good enough, I should've thought.

touch up*

A. Brand new, sir! Straight from the manufacturer!

B. But look at this door. It's been touched up.

A. Aha!

B. And this paintwork's been touched up as well.

A. Touched up, sir? Ah, yes. Yes, it has been touched up a bit here and there, sir, as you say. These modern manufacturers, sir! Aren't they dreadful, sir? I don't know! They don't seem to take a bit of care, sir, do they? Not a bit of care. Ah, well, what about this car, then, sir? How d'you like this one?

(*b*) This **door**'s been touched up.
            wing
            panel
            paintwork
            bodywork
(*a*) Touched up? Yes, it has been touched up **a bit** here and there.
                             little
                             somewhat

try out   A. No, I'm afraid that's not quite the car I'm looking for.
B. But wouldn't you like to try it out, sir? Try it out for a bit! Why not try it out? After all, there's no harm in trying it out, sir! And there's no charge for trying it out, either.
A. No, thank you. I'd rather not. It's not quite the car I'm . . .
B. Well, what about this car, sir? How d'you like this one? Wouldn't you like to try this one out, sir?

(*a*) I'm afraid that's not quite the **car** I'm looking for.
                                       model
                                       vehicle
                                       sort of thing
(*b*) But there's no harm in trying it out, sir! Try it out for **a bit**.
                                       mile or two
                                       ten minutes or so

tip off   A. They're going to rob the bank at eleven o'clock this morning, you say? Where did you get your tip-off?
B. I can't tell you who tipped me off, can I?
A. Then I can't check if the information is true, can I?
B. Well, my regular informer tipped me off, and I'm tipping you off. If you don't do anything about it, that's not my problem, is it?
A. All right – which bank?
B. All right – how much?
A. Tell me which bank, then I'll tell you how much.
B. Tell me how much, then I'll tell you which bank.

(*a*) **Where did you get your tip-off**?
     Who gave you the tip-off
     Who tipped you off
(*b*) My **regular informer** tipped me off.
     usual informant
(*a*) Tell me which **bank**.
     jeweller's
(*b*) Tell me how much.

195

turn

down (i)

A. Turn it down a bit, can't you?
B. What did you say?
A. The radio! Turn it down!
B. I can't hear you.
A. Turn that horrible, noisy music down!
B. There! Now, I'm sorry – what were you saying?
A. I was asking you to turn down the radio.
B. But I've turned it off, haven't I?

(a) Turn it down a bit, can't you?
(b) **What did you say**?
What do you say
What's that you say
What's that you're saying
What's that
What
Sorry, I can't hear you
I beg your pardon
(a) The **radio**! Turn (down) the **radio** (down)!
record player
television
tape recorder
volume

turn

down (ii)

A. But Hugh, how awful for you! I thought they said they'd accept your manuscript, and give you a job into the bargain.
B. Well, they haven't. They've turned the book down, and they've turned me down too.
A. I suppose a cup of tea wouldn't help?

(a) But **Hugh**, how **awful** for you!
dreadful
terrible
(b) They've turned (down) **the book** (down).
my manuscript
proposal
scheme
plan
suggestion
my application
(a) I suppose a **cup of tea** wouldn't help?
coffee
hot drink
whisky

196

turn
down (iii)

A. Do I look smart, mummy?
B. You look marvellous, Edward. But turn your collar down. It's sticking up at the back. Here, let me turn it down for you. There you are! Now, all ready for your first day at the big school?

(*a*) Do I look **smart**, mummy?
        all right
(*b*) You look **marvellous, Edward**. But turn (down) your collar (down).
        very smart
        splendid
        very nice
        fine

turn out
(i)*

A. Everything's turned out fine!
B. But I thought you were expecting all sorts of difficulties and all sorts of interference.
A. Well, as it turned out, the difficulties weren't as great as we'd imagined, and the interference we'd expected from various people just didn't materialize.
B. So things have actually turned out better than you'd expected?
A. Far better.
B. Of course, if I'd known it was all going to turn out so well in the end, I might've interfered a bit myself!
A. The thought had crossed my mind!

(*b*) So things have actually turned out better than you'd

  expected?
  imagined
  thought
  hoped
  feared
  ever dared to hope
          expect
          imagine
(*a*) Everything's turned out **fine**!
            splendidly
            very well indeed

turn out (ii)

A. It's a very important match. I thought there'd've been a much better turn-out than this.
B. It's poor weather, though, isn't it?
A. I blame television, you know. I mean, why should people turn out on a cold Saturday afternoon when they can watch the match on their screens?
B. We've turned out! Why shouldn't they?
A. Oh, yes, we have turned out. But then we're enthusiasts!
B. That's it. Enthusiasts, that's what we are.
A. We are. Brr! But it is poor weather, though, isn't it?

(*b*) We've turned out! Why shouldn't they?
(*a*) Oh, yes, we have turned out. But then **we're enthusiasts**.
                keen
                really keen on the game
              we haven't got television sets

turn out (iii)

A. If you're so sure you didn't take Janet's pen, perhaps you wouldn't mind turning out your pockets.
B. I haven't seen her pen, Miss Clarke.
A. Now turn out your bag. Put everything here – here, on my table.
B. Miss Clarke, I haven't seen it – I swear I haven't seen . . . Oh, Miss . . .
A. What did I say? What is that if it isn't Janet's pen? Isn't it her pen?
B. I think it is, Miss Clarke. But I didn't put it in my bag! Honestly I didn't!

(*a*) Perhaps you wouldn't mind turning out your **pockets**.
                              bag
                              satchel
                              box
                              drawer
                              locker
                              desk
                              belongings

(*b*) I haven't seen **her pen, Miss Clarke**.
             his book

turn out
(iv)

A. It's my job to turn anybody out who hasn't
   got a pass, sir. So I turned him out, sir.
B. Well, I suppose you may have done the
   right thing, Mr Strong. But you do know who
   you've just turned out, don't you?
A. No, sir. And I don't care, sir, I was only
   doing my duty, sir.
B. Even so, perhaps you will care when I tell
   you who he was.

(a) It's my **job** to turn   **anybody** out who hasn't got a **pass**.
         duty   anyone   permit
         responsibility   membership card

(b) But you do know who you've turned out, don't you?
(a) No, sir. And I don't care, sir.

turn out
(v)

A. How many of these radios do you turn out
   in a day?
B. Oh, it varies, of course. But on an average,
   we turn out about two hundred a day, and our
   other factory manages to turn out about half
   that number.
A. Well, if I may say so, you turn out a very nice
   model. I like it, I really do.
B. Good of you to say so. We do our best, you
   know.

(a) How many of these **radios** do you turn out in a **day**?
                      cars   week
                      machines   month
                      spoons
                      bottles

(b) Oh, it varies, of course. But on an average, we turn out about **two
    hundred** a day.

turn up

(i)

A. **Never mind. Perhaps a job'll turn up tomorrow.**

B. **You keep on saying that, don't you? 'Something'll turn up,' you say. 'Something's bound to turn up.' But nothing's turned up so far, has it?**

A. **Perhaps tomorrow.**

B. **Hm!**

A. **Or perhaps the next day.**

B. **Hm!**

A. **You mustn't be pessimistic. As I say . . .**

B. **'Something's bound to turn up' – you needn't say it.**

A. **Well, it is, believe me.**

(*a*) Never mind, something'll turn up **tomorrow.**

soon
before very long

(*b*) But nothing's turned up so far, has it?

turn up

(ii)

A. **Guess who's turned up to see us today.**

B. **Turned up to see us? Oh, let me see – it'll be er . . . it'll be . . . No, I'm no good at guessing. You'll have to tell me. Who has turned up?**

A. **Marion and Sara!**

B. **Marion and Sara? But I thought they were both abroad!**

A. **They've flown over for a short holiday.**

B. **Well, isn't that marvellous! How are they? Where are they? We must have a party! We must celebrate!**

A. **That's what they said themselves. They've gone out to buy something special to eat.**

B. **And I must go out and get something special to drink. After all, they don't turn up every day, do they?**

(*a*) Guess who's turned up to see us today.

(*b*) I'm **no good** at guessing. You'll have to tell me. Who has turned up?
hopeless

(*a*) **Marion and Sara.**
John and Christine
Jo and Melvyn, David and Derek

200

turn up
(iii)

A. Turn your nose up at it if you like, but that's all you're getting! I'm not going to cook anything else!

B. But you know I don't like cooked cheese, mother!

A. If it isn't one of you, it's the other. I don't know! You turn your nose up at cheese, and your brother turns his up whenever we have fish. What am I going to do with the two of you? And father won't eat vegetables.

B. Can I have some bread and butter?

A. Oh, all right! But you'll cut and butter it yourself, I can tell you!

B. Yes, mother.

A. And what am I supposed to do with all this cheese?

(*a*) You turn (up) your nose (up) at **cheese**.
                                eggs
                                potatoes
                                rice
(*b*) But you know I don't like **cheese**, mother!
(*a*) And your brother turns his up whenever we have **fish**.
                                                        chicken

use up

A. Is there any typing paper left?

B. I'm afraid it's all been used up.

A. Who's it been used up by?

B. It must've been used up by someone or other.

A. But who's used it up?

B. Somebody has.

A. But who?

B. You'd better find out, hadn't you?

A. I don't need any just at the moment, I don't think.

(*a*) Is there any **typing paper** left?
                    ink
                    soap
(*b*) I'm afraid it's all been used up.
(*a*) Are there any **drawing pins** left?
                    cleaning cloths
(*b*) I'm afraid they've all been used up.

warm up

A. We missed you at the reception.

B. To tell you the truth, I found the lecture so dull I went home before it'd finished.

A. Oh, that's a pity. The lecture itself wasn't very exciting, I agree. However, things began to warm up tremendously when the discussion began. And they warmed up even more at the reception afterwards. There was nearly a fight, actually, between the speaker and the secretary of the society.

B. A fight? A fight about the lecture?

A. Well, not, perhaps, exactly about the lecture.

(a) We missed you at the **reception**.
                  party
(b) To tell you the truth, I went home before the **lecture**'d finished.
                           talk
                           meeting
(a) Things warmed up tremendously **when the discussion began**.
                  during the discussion
                  when there were questions
                  at the reception
                        party
                  afterwards
                  later
                  later on
                  towards the end

water down (i)

A. This orange juice is terribly strong!

B. Of course it's strong – you're supposed to water it down before you drink it. If you drink it without watering it down, it's bound to taste too strong.

A. But I have watered it down!

B. Well, you'll have to water it down a bit more, then, won't you?

(b) You're supposed to water the **orange juice** down.
                  lemon squash
                  liquid
                  fluid
                  mixture
(a) But I have watered it down!
(b) Well, you'll **have to** water it down a **bit** more, **won't** you?
           must   little   mustn't

water down (ii)

A. The speech as reported in the press was only a watered-down version of the actual speech he delivered.
B. But it's supposed to be reliable. It's supposed to be a verbatim report. How was it watered down? In what way watered down?
A. Oh, yes, all the words are there. But it wasn't what he said that was so important – it was the way he said it.

(a) The **speech** as reported **in the press** was only a watered-down version.
    talk   papers
    address   newspapers
    lecture   on the news
(b) How was it watered down? In what way watered down?

wear out (i)

A. I feel worn out.
B. It's Friday. Everybody feels worn out on a Friday – that's what the weekend's for.
A. What about you? Have you had a hard day?
B. Oh, you know, the usual – cleaning, cooking, shopping, looking after the children. Nothing special.
A. You look quite worn out yourself, you know. I think what we all need is a holiday.
B. That's what I was hoping you'd say.

(a) I feel worn out.
(b) **Everyone** feels worn out **on a Friday**.
    Everybody   on Fridays
                       at the weekend
                       after a busy week
                       after a busy day
                       at the end of a long day
                       in this sort of weather
                       during this weather
                       just before the holidays

wear out (ii)

A. Everything in this factory was of the latest design.
B. Was?
A. Yes. Since Mr Graves died, nothing's been replaced. Everything's wearing out. The machines are wearing out in there, the typewriters are wearing out in here. The workers' special clothing's all worn out, and ...
B. How long've you worked here?
A. It's time I retired. It's time we all retired. It's time they trained some young people – we've all been here too long. We're like the machinery.

(a) Everything was of the latest design.
(b) Was?
(a) But now the **machines** are wearing out. Everything's wearing out.
          engines
          vehicles
          carpets

wear off

A. It didn't hurt a bit, Mr Pullar. But my mouth still feels very odd indeed.
B. That's the local anaesthetic. The funny feeling'll wear off in an hour or so. And then you'll feel a bit of soreness.
A. Which won't wear off quite so quickly!
B. Well, you have had four extractions. Yes, your mouth'll be rather sore for a day or two, I'm afraid.

(b) The funny feeling'll wear off **in an hour or so**. Then you'll feel a bit of
                          a short time
                          very soon
                          quite quickly
                          gradually
soreness.

(a) Which won't wear off quite so **quickly**!
                          soon

weigh up
(i)

A. Those are all the alternatives, all the possibilities I can think of, John. Now you must weigh them all up, and make your decision.
B. Are you sure you want me to make the decision?
A. Weigh up all the arguments, as I've said, weigh up all the pros and cons. And when you've reached a decision, I'll accept it. It's time for me to learn to accept the decisions you make.
B. Well, thank you, father. Thank you. I'll do my best.
A. And it's time for you to practise making them.

(*a*) Now you must weigh (up) the **alternatives** (up).
possibilities
arguments
evidence
pros and cons

(*b*) I'll do **my best**
very best
the best I can
the very best I can

weigh up
(ii)*

A. He's a very odd fellow in some ways.
B. What d'you mean?
A. Well, I can never quite weigh him up.
B. That's rather interesting.
A. Interesting?
B. Yes.
A. Why interesting?
B. Because he was saying the same about you. He said he couldn't weigh you up at all.
A. Just as I said – I told you he was odd.

(*a*) I can never quite weigh **the fellow up**.
girl
woman
John
him

(*b*) **He** was saying the same about you. **He** said **he** couldn't weigh you up at all.

205

while
away

A. 'Come to Happy Holiday Hotel!'
B. 'While away the hours in sunshine!'
A. 'While away the days in luxurious comfort!'
B. 'While away the weeks in magnificent surroundings!'
A. While away a wet Saturday afternoon ...
B. Reading holiday advertisements ...
A. For places we can't afford to go to anyway.

(b) While (away) **the hours** (away) in **sunshine!**'

days	comfort
time	luxury
your time	magnificent surroundings
holiday	glorious
	beautiful
	delightful
	delightful company
	elegant
	stimulating

(a) While away a **wet Saturday afternoon** ...
dreary
miserable

(b) Reading **holiday advertisements**
travel brochures

win over

A. It's a good plan.
B. Of course it's a good plan. But Gregory's against it.
A. But surely Gregory must be won over. We must persuade him to accept it.
B. Have you ever tried to win Gregory over?
A. No.
B. Ah, well, then you don't ...
A. But I'm willing to try.

(a) But surely **Gregory** can be won over.
(b) Have you ever tried **to win**   **Gregory** over? Ah, well, then you don't ...
winning
(a) But I'm **willing** to try.
prepared

wind up

(i)

A. Let me wind it up, please.
B. No. I want to wind it up.
A. It's my aeroplane!
B. Yes, it is your aeroplane.
A. So I must ...
B. But I'm going to wind it up.

(a) Let me wind it up.
(b) No. I want to wind it up.
(a) It's my **aeroplane**!
       car
       train
       clock
       watch
       musical box
(b) But I'm going to wind it up.

wind up

(ii)*

A. This was the business that Jack built up.[1]
B. This was the meeting that wound up the business that Jack built up.
A. This was the speech that wound up the meeting that wound up the business that Jack built up.
B. This was the sentence that wound up the speech that wound up the meeting that wound up the business that Jack built up.
A. This was the word that wound up the sentence that wound up the speech that wound up the meeting that wound up the business that Jack built up.
B. That was the word?
A. It was.

(b) That sentence wound up the **speech**.
                talks
                discussions
                negotiations
(a) That speech wound up the **meeting**.
                conference
                convention
(b) And the meeting wound up the **business**.
                company
                society

[1] based on 'The House that Jack built' (Nursery Rhyme)

work off

A. Twenty-two . . . twenty-three . . . twenty-four . . . twenty-five . . . There!

B. All right – so now you've done that exercise twenty-five times. But what good does it do you?

A. It works off all my spare energy, for one thing.

B. But if you have energy to spare, why don't you work it off in the garden, or cleaning the car, or at least in doing something useful.

A. Because I need all my spare energy.

B. You need it? But you just said you . . .

A. I need it for doing the exercises.

(b) Why don't you work (off) your energy (off) **in the garden**?
cutting the grass
repairing the roof
laying a new path

(a) Because I need all my spare energy for **doing exercises**.
press-ups
keeping fit

work out (i)

A. Do you think you could work out some sort of a programme of visits for our distinguished guest?

B. It's rather short notice. But I think we can probably work something out. Is he the sort who likes museums, or the sort who likes football matches?

A. Our guest is a lady, actually.

B. Oh, I see. I'm sorry. Well, of course, she . . .

A. And I think she'd probably enjoy a football match very much.

(a) Do you think you could work out some sort of **programme**?
time-table
itinerary
scheme
arrangement
plan
solution to the problem

(b) I think we can **probably** work something out.
possibly
certainly
definitely

208

work out (ii)*

A. Things haven't worked out very well for you, have they?

B. Oh, I don't complain.

A. But things have worked out rather badly, haven't they?

B. For the moment, yes. Yes, they have.

A. But you think everything might work out all right in the end?.

B. I don't merely think it will, I know it will. And now, if you don't mind, I'm rather busy.

(a) Things haven't worked out **very** well, have they?
$$\begin{array}{l} \text{so} \\ \text{too} \\ \text{at all} \end{array}$$

(b) Oh, **I don't complain**.
grumble
I'm not complaining
grumbling
I mustn't complain
grumble

(a) But things have worked out rather badly, haven't they?

(b) **For the moment**, yes.
At the moment

work out (iii)

A. Now, boys, when you've worked out those six problems, you can turn to the back of your textbooks, and there you'll find some rather intriguing mathematical puzzles.

B. What shall we do when we've worked out all the puzzles, sir?

A. When you've worked them all out, you'll be old enough and good enough to go to the university.

(a) When you've worked out the **problems**, you can work the puzzles out.
sums
equations

(b) What shall we do **when** we've worked them all out?
after

(a) **Go to the university**.
college
Take a job in a research establishment
Become a professor
Write a textbook yourself

209

work

out (iv)

A. Why did they close the mine? It wasn't completely worked out. There was still plenty of coal left in it.

B. The coal wasn't completely worked out, no. But the mine couldn't be run economically any more.

(*a*) The mine wasn't **completely** worked out.
　　　　　　　　　entirely
　　　　　　　　　altogether
　　　　　　　　　totally

(*b*) The **coal** wasn't **completely** worked out, **no**.
　　　lead　　　　　　　　　you're right
　　　copper　　　　　　　 that's true
　　　ore　　　　　　　　　 I agree
　　　seam

　　But the **gold** mine couldn't be run **economically** any **more**.
　　　　　　　　　　　　　　　　at a profit　　　longer
　　　　　　　　　　　　　　　　profitably

work

out (v)

A. If you work out the cost of the optional extras you'll see this flat's even more expensive than we imagined.

B. Yes – as I work it out, the extras cost as much as the rent itself. They're the most expensive item.

A. By the way, I can see that a mean landlord might include water among the extras. But not among the optional extras, surely!

(*a*) If you work out the **cost** of the extras, this **flat's** **more expensive**
　　　　　　　　　　　price　　　　　　　　　 house　dearer
　　　　　　　　　　　charges for　　　　　　　room
　　　　　　　　　　　　　　　　　　　　　　　 hotel
　　　　　　　　　　　　　　　　　　　　　　　 place

　　than we **imagined**.
　　　　　　thought

(*b*) As I work it out, the extras are the most expensive **item**.
　　　　　　　　　　　　　　　　　　　　　　　　　　 thing
　　　　　　　　　　　　　　　　　　　　　　　　　　 part

210

work up
(i)

A. He's a fine orator!
B. He's a fiery orator!
A. He knows how to work up a crowd.
B. Yes, he can work up a crowd's emotions all right.
A. He knows how to say things effectively.
B. Even though what he says isn't really worth saying!

(*a*) He knows how to work up **a crowd.**
                           an audience
                           his listeners
                           supporters
(*b*) Oh, yes, he can work **a crowd**'s emotions up.

work up
(ii)*

A. It's nothing serious. Don't get excited.
B. I'm not getting excited.
A. Don't get worked up.
B. I'm not getting worked up.
A. Don't get worked up about it!
B. I'm not getting worked up.
A. It's nothing at all to get worked up about!
B. You're the one that's worked up!! Calm down!!
A. I AM CALM!! I am calm.

(*a*) Don't get worked up.
(*b*) I'm not worked up.
(*a*) **It's nothing at all to get worked up about!**
    There's nothing to get worked up about
    There's no need to get worked up about it
    You don't need to get worked up
(*b*) **You're the one that's** getting worked up!
    It's you who's

work up (iii)

A. These notes are most interesting, Peter. They deserve to be worked up into a book. I'm sure a publisher would be interested.

B. I don't know about a book, but, yes, I might try to work them up into an article some time. But at the moment the immediate question is whether I can work them up into a lecture!

A. But you've fifteen minutes yet! Plenty of time!

B. Ha ha!

(a) These **notes deserve to be** worked up into a book.
       ideas need
         ought
         should be

(b) I might try to work them up into **an article**   **some time**.
                    a paper   when I have time
                       dissertation   if I have time
                       thesis
                       broadcast talk

write off (i)*

A. It was a tremendous explosion. Most of the machinery in that room'll have to be written off completely. The drilling machine, for instance – that's a complete write-off.

B. Most of the machinery needed writing off long before the explosion.

A. Yes, I suppose an explosion was just about the only way of getting new machinery from this management.

B. Quite.

(a) Most of the **machinery** will have to be written off.
                equipment
                stock
                stores
                machines
                tools
                books
                spare parts
                damaged goods

(b) Most of **it** needed **writing off**.
           them   to be written off

212

write

off (ii)

A. I say – they're giving away free samples. I think I'll write off for one.
B. I've written off for one already.
A. You've written off to this address?
B. Yes.
A. For a free sample?
B. That's it.
A. From this address?
B. Of course.
A. But they won't send more than one sample to each address!
B. I suppose there is just time for you to find somewhere else to live before the offer closes.

(a) I think I'll write off for **a free sample**.
pamphlet
brochure
prospectus
some information
more details

(b) I've **written off already**.
already written off

write

out (i)*

A. Do you write your speeches out in full, or do you work from notes entirely?
B. Oh, I write them out in full. In fact, I often write out several versions. What about you?
A. Oh, I make my speeches first, and write them out afterwards.
B. Why bother to write them out afterwards?
A. As an accurate record of what I wish I'd said!

(a) Do you write (out) your **speeches** (out) in full?
reports
stories
replies
talks
answers

(b) I **often** write out **several** versions.
frequently   a few
usually   one or two
occasionally a number of

213

write out (ii)

A. He's written twelve novels. That's quite a large output for one so young.
B. But the last two were rather poor, I thought. In fact I reckon he's just about written himself out.
A. They weren't very good, I agree. But I don't think he's written out yet, by any means. No, I think he'll still be writing good novels even ten years from now.
B. Of course, you're his publisher, you have to believe in him.
A. I'm his sternest critic – and his friend – and I do believe in him.

(b) I **reckon** he's just about written himself out.
    think
(a) I don't **think** he's written out yet, **by any means**.
    reckon   by a long way
                      by a long chalk

write out (iii)

A. To have played the same part in a radio serial for eight years is quite an accomplishment.
B. Even so, I'm tired of being Uncle Rupert. I'm not a bit like him at all, and I'm hoping to get a different kind of part in a stage play, or on TV, or in a film – anything for a change. They're going to write me out next month.
A. Write you out? Uncle Rupert's going to be written out? After eight years? But what will they do with Uncle Rupert?
B. Send him abroad, perhaps.
A. Or perhaps kill him off? Poor Uncle Rupert!
B. As long as they write me out of the serial, they can do what they like with Uncle Rupert!

(b) They're going to write me out **of the serial**.
                             play
                            series
                in the next episode
(a) Write you out? **Uncle Rupert**'s going to be written out?
    Aunt Millicent

write up

(i)

A. I missed the lecture today. Did you go?

B. Yes. Actually, it was very good.

A. Do you think I could borrow your notes?

B. I haven't written them up, yet – and you wouldn't be able to read the rough notes I took.

A. But when you have written them up, may I?

B. Of course – but I shan't be writing them up until after that cup of coffee you promised me!

(*b*) I haven't written (up) my **notes** (up) yet.
  lecture notes
  rough notes

(*a*) May I **borrow** them when you have written them up?
  look at
  see
  copy

(*b*) Of course.

write up

(ii)

A. I think I'll write to the publisher about these conversations.

B. Yes, write up and tell them what you think.

A. Though, I suppose if I do write up, they won't take any notice.

B. They might – you never know. Why not write up anyway?

A. All right – I will!

(*a*) I'll write to the **publisher** about them.
  author
  editor

(*b*) Yes, write up and tell them **what you think**.
  your opinion
  views
  impressions

(*a*) I suppose they won't **take any notice**.
  pay any attention

(*b*) Why not write up anyway?